T0268464

SEEING GOD IN DIVERSITY
Exodus and Acts

Elizabeth M. Magill and Angela Bauer-Levesque

Commissioned by the Anti-Racism Committee of the
Executive Council of the Episcopal Church

MOREHOUSE PUBLISHING

HARRISBURG / PENNSYLVANIA

Morehouse Publishing, P.O. Box 1321, Harrisburg, PA 17105

Morehouse Publishing, The Tower Building, 11 York Road, London SE1 7NX

Morehouse Publishing is a Continuum imprint.

Cover design by Wesley Hoke

Library of Congress Cataloging-in-Publication Data

Magill, Elizabeth M.
    Seeing God in diversity : Exodus and Acts / Elizabeth M. Magill and Angela Bauer-Levesque.
        p.   cm.
    "Commissioned by the Anti-Racism Committee of the Executive Council of the Episcopal Church."
    Includes bibliographical references (p.   ).
    ISBN-13: 978-0-8192-2160-5 (pbk.)
    1. Reconciliation—Biblical teaching.   2. Reconciliation—Religious aspects—Christianity.
3. Bible. O.T. Exodus—Criticism, interpretation, etc.   4. Bible. N.T. Acts—Criticism, interpretation, etc.   5. Bible. O.T. Exodus—Study and teaching.   6. Bible. N.T. Acts—Study and teaching.
I. Bauer-Levesque, Angela, 1960-   II. Title.
BS1245.6.R35M34   2006
234'.5—dc22

                                                                                            2005025423

Printed in the United States of America

01 02 03 04 05 06 07 08 09   10 9 8 7 6 5 4 3 2 1

CONTENTS

ACKNOWLEDGMENTS

This work was commissioned by the Anti-Racism Committee of the Executive Council of the Episcopal Church, Sheryl A. Kujawa-Holbrook, chair. Jayne J. Oasin of the Social Justice Ministries Office of the Episcopal Church, 815 Second Avenue, New York, New York 10017, www.episcopalchurch.org, provided financial support for the publication.

Individuals, congregations, and dioceses interested in additional anti-racism resources should contact the Social Justice Ministries Office for further information.

Special thanks to Debra Farrington, Ryan Masteller, and Morehouse Publishing for their support and enthusiasm for this project.

A grant from the Conant Fund of the Episcopal Church Foundation supported Dr. Angela Bauer-Levesque's initial work on this project; its completion was made possible by a sabbatical grant from the Lilly Theological Research Grants Program through the Association of Theological Schools.

FOREWORD

Dear Friends,

Anti-racism is hard work at best, frustrating and thankless work at its worst. I have been a professional trainer for over twenty-five years engaged in a variety of training topics and settings ranging from nonprofit strategic planning, to customer service for the banking industry, to fund raising and mission development for churches. I could hold most of those issues outside of myself, even when I was deeply interested in the topic. But now I work on issues of racism in society and in the church on a daily basis and I can no longer keep the issues at bay. Working with people on issues surrounding racism requires all that I have and all that I am.

As I work in anti-racism ministries across the Episcopal Church, often I have asked myself (and I know that I am not alone in asking this question) where to go for strength and help. We hope that God, with gracious mercy, will look deeply into our hearts torn apart with fear, anger, guilt, and resentment because of racism—whether we are victims or perpetrators. Enter God, we pray, search out the deeply sinful and painful places of our hearts. Cleanse us as only you can do and make us whole. Enter into the daily pain of our human existence and bring in the peace that passes all understanding and, after having done so, send us back out into the broken and unjust world "in peace to love and serve the Lord." This we cannot do alone.

After more than six years of focus on anti-racism training throughout the Episcopal Church, the Anti-Racism Committee of the Executive Council decided that it was time to commission some further resources for adult education in congregations. The national committee commissioned this study guide in an attempt to provide people an opportunity to reflect on racism within the context of scripture. Thanks to Dr. Angela Bauer-Levesque of the Episcopal Divinity School and the Reverend Elizabeth M. Magill, a certified anti-racism trainer, we hope this resource will provide a challenging and supportive opportunity to engage an important issue within your congregation. For additional anti-racism resources, please contact the Social Justice Ministries Office at the Episcopal Church Center, www.episcopalchurch.org.

May God, who has given us the will to work for a just world, give us the strength and determination to create models within our beloved church for the communities in which we live.

> Faithfully,
> The Reverend Jayne J. Oasin
> Social Justice Officer
> The Episcopal Church Center
> Ash Wednesday 2005

INTRODUCTION

The resource you are holding, *Seeing God in Diversity: Exodus and Acts,* is an adult resource for parishes who want to explore the Bible faithfully. We are suggesting that there is good news in scripture for the reader—and that the good news is different depending on which character we identify with. Indeed, where we find good news depends on the lenses—the perspectives—we use when we read scripture.

The characters in our reading are many and diverse. From the exercise of identifying with new characters, we hope that participants will discover that the *social location* of all readers—specifically, who we are with a particular racial, ethnic, and cultural heritage—influences not only how we read scripture, but also how we read and understand our community. What we see in our church, in our neighborhood, and in the world depends on and is prejudiced by the lenses we are wearing.

Prejudice is not something we must accept. We can choose to hear each other's stories, taste another culture, see a different point of view; we can choose to be touched by the diversity around us. But to reject prejudice we must risk admitting that our view is not the only view, nor the best view, and that it certainly is incomplete. The risk in this study is that we may discover that our call, our response to Christ, the good news that we are to proclaim to the nations, may be very different from what we thought. And it might involve very hard work.

This book uses the biblical stories found in Exodus and Acts to help participants explore the richness of stories told from a variety of perspectives. In the sessions that follow, participants will be asked to think about the stories from the different viewpoints of the various characters in the stories and, in doing so, to broaden their own understanding of scripture.

Pointers for leading these sessions follow in the next chapter, along with some background on the books of Exodus and Acts. As the group leader, you will find it helpful to read the biblical books in advance of the program. If it seems constructive to do so, you may also want to consult some basic commentaries on the two books.

We strongly urge you to make all background materials on the Bible available to the participants of the study, especially the introduction. Ideally, all participants will have their own copies of this resource.

LEADING THE STUDY

The *Seeing God in Diversity* study guide is designed to work within six two-hour sessions. The study follows a set format for each session: 1) worship, 2) setting the tone, 3) finding perspective, 4) considering the text, and 5) closing concerns and prayer. The program can easily be adapted to twelve shorter sessions or for a weekend retreat.

Create shorter meetings by splitting each session into part A and part B. Use the *opening worship* and the *ground rules* each time you meet, but leave out the sharing from the worship for part A. Spend the allotted time on *setting the tone* only in part A, but be sure the ground rules are posted and acknowledged at each meeting. Skip *finding perspective* in part B. When *considering the text*, read the scripture aloud in part A, and begin the discussion, but leave the commentaries and the heart of the discussion to part B. This material will work best if you allow an hour and fifteen minutes for each session.

The optimal retreat schedule requires twelve hours of study plus break time and meals. A closing Eucharist could repeat the sharing from the first session. Gathering for worship and an early dinner and continuing through lunch on the third day works well, as does scheduling two eight-hour days. It is important to maintain the flow of *finding perspective* and *considering the text* as written in this guide. While *worship* is the heart of this program, the timing is flexible. Move the services as necessary to fit the meal and break schedule. After the opening discussion of *setting the tone*, be prepared to use one of the follow-up discussions as needed, and keep the ground rules posted throughout the event. Simply pointing them out after breaks and meals is one way to keep them in participants' minds. If discussions get heated, turn to the *setting the tone* discussion from session two or three. Be prepared to adjust your plans as you gauge the comfort of the group.

Facilitation skills and the ability to create an environment where participants feel comfortable enough to share difficult thoughts and feelings are more important than scholarly biblical knowledge for the leaders of this study as found in commentaries. While all should read the background provided on Exodus and Acts, the heart of the study will be challenging the group to consider each text from a fresh perspective. When participants provide pat and comfortable answers, push the group to go deeper. Help each person consider who he or she is in the world, and who he or she might be in the text presented. Accept all answers and then ask for more.

WORSHIP helps the group prepare to be open and receptive to God and to each other. We are not studying algebra; we are looking for God's good news to us in the world. The worship structure and opening and closing prayers remain the same each week, while the scripture, sharing, and music change. Hymn suggestions are listed for each week. The hymns come from Episcopal hymnals available in many parishes: The Hymnal 1982 (H1982); *Lift Every Voice and Sing* (LEVAS II); and *Wonder, Love & Praise* (WLP). If singing from the hymnal is difficult, bring in a CD with appropriate music for the worship.

Consider inviting a different person to lead the worship each week, reinforcing the diversity of voices that is at the core of this program. Worship is also about sharing who we are, and so a question for participants to answer is part of each week's worship. Allow a minute for each person the first week; you will need more time, perhaps two or three minutes per person, in later weeks. If you have a large group, you may find it helpful to have them share in small groups of three to four people each. Make sure that participants know that it is always okay to pass if they don't want to speak.

In the first week, participants will share a personal item from their cultural, racial, or ethnic heritage. As the leader, be prepared to go first if needed. In the second week, they describe their heritage. In week three, all will share what they are most proud of from their heritage. Some will find this question difficult to answer. Remind people that they are welcome to pass. In week four, individuals will talk about the first time they realized that there were different racial, ethnic, or cultural backgrounds, and if they noticed that they were treated differently because of their background. During worship in week five, participants will remember the childhood lessons they learned about difference; in week six, the group will imagine what the world would be like if we hadn't learned to treat one another differently.

SETTING THE TONE will be essential to the study. Present the ground rules provided at the start of the study (see pages 3-4), and mention them again each week. Notice and gently correct instances where people cross the line. After the first week, be sure to allow time for people to bring up concerns that occurred to them since the last session. Make space for people to talk about how they are feeling.

FINDING PERSPECTIVE is an effort to learn in a more "right-brained" way. The exercises are designed to promote discussion and creative thinking and to challenge participants in new ways. The activities are meant to be fun and should be treated lightly. There are *no* wrong answers!

CONSIDERING THE TEXT invites participants to delve more deeply into the text itself. Some weeks this involves reading some of the biblical text aloud, and other weeks we've provided a readers' theater version of the scripture. Don't let the group get caught up worrying about the quality of the dramatic reading. The goal is not a full-scale acting out, but rather to hear the text in many voices. If your group is small, a person may read more than one part of the text. Questions for discussion are provided each week. Allow the group time to respond to the questions before moving to the commentary provided.

CLOSING CONCERNS AND PRAYER is a wrap-up of the session. Ask the participants: What have you learned? What are you wondering about? How is everyone feeling? If there has been disagreement in the session, check with those involved to be sure that everyone is okay. Remind the group that we don't have to agree with each other or with this book. We *do* need to pray together!

INTRODUCTION TO EXODUS AND THE ACTS OF THE APOSTLES

Exodus

Exodus is a story of beginnings, the beginning of a unique and holy people. It is also the story of the beginning of a covenant relationship between the people and their God YHWH, whom they worship. While there were covenants in the Bible between individuals and God before the book of Exodus begins, this is the first covenant between God and a people. The book of Exodus is part of Torah, which is often translated as "the Law." While it includes legal materials, Torah is much more than just rules and regulations. It is instruction on how to live faithfully in community. In the Septuagint, the earliest Greek translation of the Hebrew Bible, Exodus was called *exhodos*, which means "the way out." In Hebrew, Exodus is called *Shemoth*, "Names," from the first line of the first chapter: "These are the names . . ." (*we'elleh shemoth bene yisrael*). The title highlights the power of naming in the making of community.

To familiarize yourself with how the story of a people develops, it is helpful to read Exodus 1 through 15, which you should do during the week by yourselves at home. The story begins with the midwives Shiprah and Puah, Moses' sister (later known as Miriam), and Pharaoh's daughter and her attendants saving the life of baby Moses. The story follows Moses as he grows up at the Egyptian court but then flees Egypt. God then reveals Godself to Moses in the burning bush and calls him to lead the people out of enslavement in Egypt. Our section of Exodus concludes with the story of the ten plagues and the Passover, the departure from Egypt, and the celebration of the crossing of the Sea of Reeds.

Historical Background

As you know, the books of the Bible were not written simultaneously with the people's experience. The stories persisted in oral tradition and were not written down until several hundred years later. Scholars date the writing from sometime between the tenth and sixth centuries BCE, while the stories themselves reference much earlier times. Indeed, there is no evidence outside the Bible thus far that the Hebrew people were ever in Egypt. A few records from Egypt mention foreigners in Egypt. Some official correspondence between Egyptian pharaohs and their vassals all over the world, known as the *Amarna Letters*, mention a group of people called *Habiru/Hapiru/Apiru*. They were considered fugitives from their own countries living at the margins of society. You can hear similarities to the word "Hebrews," and perhaps the *Habiru* were some of their ancestors.

During the thirteenth century BCE, during the nineteenth dynasty of the Egyptian pharaohs, Rameses (Raameses) II (1290–1224 or 1304–1237) came to power. It is likely that he is the pharaoh found in Exodus 1:8: "Now a new king arose over Egypt, who did not know Joseph...." Yet the Bible does not tell us his name. Keep in mind how names embody power and signify a variety of meanings within their context.

We will explore this story from Exodus from three different perspectives: 1) the perspective of the Hebrews, with whom the narra-

tor of Exodus identifies and whom we know best from our previous
encounters with the book; 2) the perspective of the Canaanites, into
whose land the Hebrews who become known as the Israelites come
looking for their liberation; and finally 3) from the perspective of
the Egyptians, who represent the empire from which God's people
are escaping.

The Acts of the Apostles

The Acts of the Apostles reads like a history of the early church, but
it is unlikely that that was the author's intent. The writer, tradition-
ally called Luke and likely the same person who wrote the Gospel of
Luke, addressed the tract to Theophilus, apparently a Greek convert
to the Christian faith. Written in around 85 CE, the story speaks of
the growth of the Christian movement and includes a great deal of
detail about Paul's success in the mission to the Gentiles.

While many of the Lucan texts are in the first person, implying
the writer traveled with Paul, he does not seem to know about Paul's
letters to the churches. In addition, many of the details fail to coin-
cide with Paul's own descriptions in his letters.

Scholars usually describe this book as historiography: a collec-
tion of events and stories organized and edited to support Luke's
theological message. As a child, I learned that Acts is the story of
how two diverse and even antagonistic traditions, Judaism and
paganism, find unity and shared meals through the Christian faith.
Indeed, the triumph of Christianity in the face of many trials is certainly one point of the book. Many of the stories show the benefits
of perseverance and boldness in faith. Interestingly, scholars are
divided on whether the text is more focused on maintaining Christianity's ties with our Jewish roots or proving to the Romans that
Christianity is not a threat.

What is relevant in this study is the struggle in Acts to create a
new community out of an old one. The disciples, all Jews, begin with
the idea that Jesus has come to the Jewish community to save it.
Slowly, the community realizes that all the Jews are not going to
accept Jesus as the messiah predicted in scripture. Just as slowly, the

community becomes aware that the Holy Spirit's presence is not limited to people from one ethnic or religious heritage.

The Holy Spirit challenged the new Christians as they attempted to define what it meant to follow Christ and eventually what it meant to be a new faith community. Which rules from their past should they carry forward? Which old behaviors were important to retain, and what new behaviors were expected? In what way did Christianity differ from Judaism?

The boundaries of the new community are still porous in the Acts of the Apostles. The community has not yet determined who is in or who is out. They have not yet distinguished between the leaders and the followers. In fact, they haven't drawn very many boundaries at all.

As these new Christians are coming to understand that they are not a Jewish community, the very concept of the nation of Israel is under threat. The Roman world of 80 CE was not a wonderful time to be Jewish. While the Roman Empire generally ruled its occupied territories with local leaders, when the Jews revolted against Roman rule in 66 CE, Rome responded by crushing the nation, destroying the temple, and ending local governance. By 70 CE, Jerusalem, the center of Jewish faith and national identity, was destroyed and recreated as a pagan city. The continuance of Judaism was not certain at all. Jewish leaders fled and were scattered throughout the empire. As Jewish hopes that insurrection would lead to self-rule were dashed, the Christians were preaching that their Savior predicted the destruction of the temple and called all to a new faith. The Acts of the Apostles is the story of the conflict of the Jews of the Diaspora (who have maintained their distinct identity from the pagans around them by strict sexual codes and synagogue worship) with the Christians, who are filling the synagogues and bringing pagan converts to eat and worship with them.

Exodus and Acts

We chose Exodus and the Acts of the Apostles for this study because they are foundational stories in the traditions of the Christian faith: the formation of the people of God in Exodus and the formation of

the early church in Acts. These two faith communities take journeys
that lead to diverse communities, new cultures, and a different way
of life. In many ways, today's congregations are struggling to take
these same journeys—leaving behind a life of oppression for the
promises of the kingdom of God, like the story of Exodus, and join-
ing disparate cultures into one Christian community, as in the Acts
of the Apostles.

And yet, over time, we have developed a limited view of these
stories. By assuming always that the story is only speaking to the
Israelites in Exodus and only to the Christians in Acts, we are miss-
ing part of God's word to the community. Exodus and Acts have been
foundational to our faith, and they still have more to offer us if we
look deeper into the texts.

SESSION ONE:
WHAT IS PERSPECTIVE?

Before the Session

Invite participants to bring an item that reminds them of their cultural, ethnic, or racial heritage for the worship activity. In addition, participants should scan Exodus 1-15. They should also read the background material on Exodus from the introduction.

Leader Preparation

- Reread the background material on Exodus, as well as Exodus 1-15, particularly Exodus 15:1-21, in preparation for section 4 below.
- Set up a worship space with room for a Bible, a cross, candles, and other objects meaningful to your congregation. Allow ample space for displaying items related to people's cultural, ethnic, or racial heritages.
- Make sure that the meeting space is flexible and large enough that chairs can be moved around to accommodate both large and small group discussion.
- Make sure there are enough bibles for everyone in the group, or ask people to bring bibles with them.
- If desired, make sure that coffee, tea, or other beverages are available for break periods.

- Mark the scripture passage, Deuteronomy 26:5-9, and choose a hymn or set up a CD player for music. Before the session begins, assign participants readings for worship time.
- Make copies of the story in the FINDING PERSPECTIVE section. Make enough copies so that small groups of three to four people will each have at least one copy of the story.

Suggested Outline for Session One

1. Opening worship (10 minutes)
2. Setting the tone: ground rules (5 minutes)
3. Finding perspective (25 minutes)
4. Considering scripture: Exodus (60 minutes)
5. Closing concerns and prayer (5-10 minutes)

Details of Session One

Worship

LEADER: The Lord be with you
PEOPLE: and also with you
LEADER: Let us pray.
We gather together, Lord, to share your word with one another. Guide us in our reading, in our studying, in our sharing, and guide us, dear God, in our listening to each other, and to you. Teach us to hear your word, and to live your word, with all our hearts, with all our souls, with all our minds. Amen.

Scripture: Deuteronomy 26:5-9

LEADER: All are invited to share of themselves during this study. Please come forward now with the item you have brought. Share your name and a sentence or two about why this item is important to you.

Singing: Choose a song about liberation that is familiar to your group. If you do not have a song leader in the study, consider playing a CD.

Go Down, Moses (LEVAS 228)
Oh, Freedom! (LEVAS 225)
We shall overcome (LEVAS 227)

Closing Prayer: ALL: O God, who created all peoples in your image, we thank you for the wonderful diversity of races and cultures in this world. Enrich our lives by ever-widening circles of fellowship, and show us your presence in those who differ most from us, until our knowledge of your love is made perfect in our love for all your children, through Jesus Christ our Lord. Amen. (BCP, p. 840)

Once the group is settled, even before introductions, use the ground rules[1] to set the tone for your study. Let participants know that these particular ground rules will help create a space within which conversation—even risky conversation—can happen honestly. Remind them that this study touches on topics that are heartfelt and perhaps difficult to discuss, so the ground rules are important. Read them out loud and get cooperation from each person by giving each member of the group an opportunity to respond to the ground rules, ask questions, etc. Ask participants if there are any additions that would help to create a space for comfortable conversation. Keep copies of the ground rules available for every session or post a large version in your room.

Finding Perspective

The next part of the session provides an opportunity for people to get involved personally with the week's theme. Let the group know that you are going to read a very short story to them and then ask them to break up into small groups to work with the story. It can be helpful to break them into groups before reading the story so that the movement around the room doesn't cause people to forget what they've heard.

---

1. Adapted from *Seeing the Face of God in Each Other: An Anti-Racism Training Manual* (New York: Episcopal Church Center, 2003), pp. 53-54.

- Break into groups of two to four people and hand out a copy of "A Story of an Executive" to each group. Assign each group a different role: Executive, Police Officer, Homemaker. Each group should listen to the story from the perspective of his or her assigned character. If your study has fewer than six participants, some persons may take a role by themselves, or do the

Ground Rules

We are each responsible for ourselves: our primary commitment is to learn and gain understanding from the study leaders, from each other, from the study guide, and from our experience.

We will not blame or shame others or ourselves: we assume that each person is doing his or her best to participate in the dialogue.

We will appreciate how we are different: we assume that each person's experience is an honest reflection of his or her lens, and that each of us has had different life experiences.

We will try something new: our study is about seeing old texts from a new perspective. We will try to understand the new way of seeing before trying to prove that it is wrong.

We will practice dialogue rather than debate: we are not looking for one right answer. We will listen more and explain less. We will look for places of agreement and concentrate on paying attention to our feelings as well as those of others. Dialogue allows room for silence and individuals may always choose to pass.

We will respect confidentiality: we agree to respect confidentiality when it is requested and to request confidentiality when we need it. We will not repeat another person's story without his or her permission.

exercise as a whole group three times, once for each role. If you are working with a large group, let several different groups cover the same character rather than making the groups larger.

- Give the groups about fifteen minutes to rewrite the story from the perspective of their assigned character. Ask them to develop a story that has a happy ending from their character's viewpoint. They cannot change the details provided, but they may add details, descriptions, other events, dialogue, and explanations where necessary. Let the small groups know that you will be asking them to share their stories with the whole group.
- Stop after fifteen minutes even if some groups have not completed the assignment. Allow each group to talk about its role and to tell the story it created in a creative way.
- After the small groups have shared their stories, involve the entire group in discussion using the questions below.

A Story of an Executive

An executive is walking home after a bad day at work. Focusing on frustration with an incompetent manager, the executive takes a wrong turn and does not notice the neighborhood is of a different ethnic heritage than that of the planned route.

A police officer startles the executive by offering to help. A quick explanation is all that is needed to send the police officer back to work, but the executive can't help wonder what prompted the question, and how long the police officer had been watching.

Arriving home, the executive is met by the family homemaker, who says that dinner will be late this evening due to an earlier crisis. The executive swears, slams down a briefcase and newspaper, and stamps out of the house.

Discussion Questions

1. How did the stories that the groups came up with differ? How were they the same?
2. How does the character telling the story influence the story and the definition of a "happy ending"?

Considering Scripture, Exodus 15:1-21

In this section, work with the group on reading and understanding the story in Exodus 15:1-21. Read the story aloud or ask someone in the group to read it, and then engage the group in conversation using the questions below. Try to keep the group focused on appreciating the richness of the diverse approaches from the various study participants as well as the connections between how people understand or interpret the story.

Discussion Questions

1. What is celebrated in this story?
2. Imagine you are among the Hebrews. What does the story tell you about yourselves, your God, your neighbors?

As your ending time nears or as the discussion begins to quiet down, you may find it helpful to summarize some of the diversity as well as the points of similarity or connection heard during the conversation. Let the group know what the following week's reading assignment is. Close the session with the prayer below.

Closing Concerns and Prayer
(based on Exodus 15:11-13)

Let your right hand, O LORD, glorious in power, guide us in our journey. In the greatness of your majesty, overthrow those who stop us from living your way. Who is like you, O LORD, majestic in holiness, awesome in splendor, doing wonders? In your steadfast love, lead us, the people you have redeemed, guide us by your strength to your holy abode. Bring us to the sanctuary that you have established. Let us sing to the LORD who triumphs gloriously! Amen.

SESSION TWO:
A CHRISTIAN PERSPECTIVE: ACTS

Before the Session

Participants should read Acts 6:1–8:2 before this session, as well as the background on Acts from the introduction. If you are not able to keep your study space intact from week to week, follow the preparation procedures from week one again.

- Mark the scripture passage, Joel 2:28–29. Choose a hymn or set up the CD player.
- Reread the background on Acts at the beginning of this chapter and be prepared to summarize that information as needed during the CONSIDERING SCRIPTURE section of today's session.
- Assign two people to read Stephen's words as well as one person to be the council and another to be the narrator. Make photocopies of the readers' theater in this session for the readers.
- Gather news magazines or newspapers, one for every three or four participants. Provide several pairs of scissors for each group. Glue, tape, and poster board are optional.

Suggested Outline for Session Two

1. Opening worship (20 minutes)
2. Setting the tone (10 minutes)
3. Finding perspective (25 minutes)
4. Considering scripture:Acts (60 minutes)
5. Closing concerns and prayer (5-10 minutes)

Details of Session Two

Worship

LEADER:The Lord be with you
PEOPLE: and also with you
LEADER: Let us pray.
We gather together, Lord, to share your word with one another. Guide us in our reading, in our studying, in our sharing, and guide us, dear God, in our listening to each other, and to you.Teach us to hear your word, and to live your word, with all our hearts, with all our souls, with all our minds.Amen.

Scripture:Joel 2:28-29

LEADER: Tell us briefly about your ethnic, racial, or cultural heritage.
[Note to the leader: try to limit each person's contribution so that you don't exceed the twenty minutes allocated for worship. If you have a large group, break into smaller groups for this time of sharing.]

Singing: Choose a song about the Holy Spirit that is familiar to your group. If you do not have a song leader in the study, consider playing a CD.

Spirit of the Living God (LEVAS 115)
Every Time I Feel the Spirit (LEVAS 114)
Breathe on Me Breath of God (H1982 508)

Santo, Santo, Santo (WLP 785)
Sweet, Sweet Spirit (WLP 752)

Closing Prayer: ALL: O God, who created all peoples in your image, we thank you for the wonderful diversity of races and cultures in this world. Enrich our lives by ever-widening circles of fellowship, and show us your presence in those who differ most from us, until our knowledge of your love is made perfect in our love for all your children; through Jesus Christ our Lord. Amen. (BCP, p. 840.)

Setting the Tone

Remind the group of the ground rules and ask how they are feeling about using them. Consider adding additional rules if necessary.

Ask the group to focus on one particular ground rule, saying, "We will try something new." Use the following questions to guide the conversation:

- What is hard about trying new things?
- What do you need in order to be able try a new idea?

Close this part of the session by reminding people that these sessions are composed of dialogue, not debate. Encourage them to continue trying to look at things in new ways. Participants can try out new ways of looking at things and then decide later that they don't like a given perspective. Trying it is not a commitment to liking it!

Finding Perspective: Who Looks Good?

Divide the group into smaller groups of three to four people each, and give each group one or more newspapers or news magazines. Ask the members to cut the source up and divide the stories and pictures into two piles: those who are getting "good press" and those who are getting "bad press." Let each group decide for themselves exactly what that means. If your group has creative energy, encourage them to divide a poster board in half and make two collages with the "good" and the "bad" stories. (20 minutes)

When the groups have finished, ask them to share their results or to show their collages. After each group has had a chance to present, lead the large group in conversation using the questions below.

Discussion Questions

1. What race or ethnic heritage predominates in the good press lists?
2. What race or ethnic heritage predominates in the bad press lists?
3. Do these lists of groups getting good and bad press provide an accurate picture of your community? Why or why not?

Considering Scripture, Acts 7:48-60

Give the group some background on today's readings from Acts. Set the stage most particularly with the events in Acts 6-7:48 that lead up to today's readers theater. You can use the following introductions to the various characters to help set the stage.

An Introduction to the Characters

All of the characters in today's scripture understand themselves to be Jewish. Stephen was a *Hellenistic Jew* who follows the Messiah, Jesus. Hellenists were Jews of the Diaspora, whose culture and formal language was Greek, though they also spoke the local language of their community. Since the story takes place in Jerusalem, Stephen must have been visiting the city in order to worship or to trade. His family would have been one of the many Jewish families that settled throughout the Roman Empire for generations. Aramaic, the spoken language of Palestine, would be a foreign tongue; he would have known the Jewish scriptures in Greek, from the translation called the Septuagint.

Stephen is in front of the council in Jerusalem; that is, the *Jewish leaders*. In Jerusalem, the leaders of the faith were the political leaders of the community until 70 CE, when Rome destroyed the temple and instituted their own leadership. Elders, scribes, and the high priest are mentioned as part of the council. The role of high priest would disappear once there was no temple worship; however, the council's authority over the faith is still clearly strong in this story.

Jewish leaders in this story are *Palestinian Jews*, referred to in Acts as Hebrews. While the local tongue was Aramaic, the liturgical language was Hebrew. Jesus and all of his disciples were Palestinian Jews; the first Hellenistic converts were made in Acts 2, on Pentecost.

Acts 7:48-60

STEPHEN ONE: "Yet the Most High does not dwell in houses made with human hands; as the prophet says,

STEPHEN TWO: 'Heaven is my throne, and the earth is my footstool. What kind of house will you build for me, says the Lord, or what is the place of my rest? Did not my hand make all these things?'

STEPHEN ONE: "You stiff-necked people, uncircumcised in heart and ears, you are forever opposing the Holy Spirit, just as your ancestors used to do. Which of the prophets did your ancestors not persecute? They killed those who foretold the coming of the Righteous One, and now you have become his betrayers and murderers. You are the ones that received the law as ordained by angels, and yet you have not kept it."

COUNCIL: When they heard these things, they became enraged and ground their teeth at Stephen.

NARRATOR: But filled with the Holy Spirit, he gazed into heaven and saw the glory of God and Jesus standing at the right hand of God.

STEPHEN TWO: "Look," he said, "I see the heavens opened and the Son of Man standing at the right hand of God!"

COUNCIL: But they covered their ears, and with a loud shout all rushed together against him. Then they dragged him out of the city and began to stone him; and the witnesses laid their coats at the feet of a young man named Saul. While they were stoning Stephen, he prayed,

STEPHEN ONE:"Lord Jesus, receive my spirit."

STEPHEN TWO:Then he knelt down and cried out in a loud voice, "Lord, do not hold this sin against them."

NARRATOR:When he had said this, he died.

At the end of the reading, lead a discussion of the passage using the following questions as discussion starters.

Discussion Questions

1. What behavior is honored?
2. Imagine you are among the Christians. What does the story tell you about yourselves, your God, your neighbors?

Commentary on Acts 15:1–21 as Background

Watch for the presence of the Holy Spirit throughout this study! In Acts 6, the story of Stephen starts with early congregational conflict. The location is Jerusalem; the new Christian community is growing rapidly. Remember from Acts 2 how the Holy Spirit is firing up people from diverse ethnic and language heritages. The use of the words "Hellenists" and "Hebrews" in the opening passage likely is a reference to language. In this context, "Hellenists" are not pagan converts, but rather Jews of the Diaspora. They live in different communities throughout the Roman Empire, speak local languages rather than the Aramaic of Jerusalem, and have returned to Jerusalem for worship or trade.

The Aramaic-speaking Apostles, that is, the "locals," resolve the conflict by expanding authoritative leadership to these Greek-speaking Jewish Christians of the Diaspora. Stephen, full of faith and the Holy Spirit, performs wonders and signs and quickly experiences conflict with other Greek-speaking Jews of the Diaspora. He is brought to a tribunal that is probably composed of Aramaic-speaking Jewish leaders.

The tribunal accuses Stephen of blasphemy against Moses and God. Blasphemy against God is punishable by death; blasphemy against Moses is not actually a crime. Stephen's speech is essentially a retelling of the story of the Israelites who heard and disobeyed God's messengers. At first, it seems the speech is a recital of God's working in history, but it quickly becomes obvious that this is an indictment of the faith of members of the tribunal. Throughout the generations, the people of God are offered salvation and instead reject the messenger. Stephen's speech builds two cases: Jesus is clearly a part of God's long-time covenant with the Israelites, and the rejection of Jesus is a continuation of the rejection of Moses and the prophets. To further offend this group of temple leaders, Stephen adds that the temple, recently destroyed, is not, in fact, where God resides.

Thus says the LORD:
Heaven is my throne
and the earth is my footstool;
what is the house that you would build for me,
and what is my resting place? (Isaiah 66:1)

While the charge of blasphemy is false, it is clear that Stephen is attacking what the tribunal holds dear. He charges his accusers with being stiff-necked, uncircumcised in their hearts, opposed to the Holy Spirit, and rejecting Jesus Christ. In that, he claims, the men of the tribunal have failed to keep the law of Moses.

This scene appears to be taking place in a court of law, yet there is no verdict. What started as an orderly trial is now described by Luke as a mob scene. The accusers are enraged; Stephen is calmly watching Jesus, the prophet they rejected, who sits in the heavens at the right hand of God. Although Stephen's countercharges parallel the tribunal's charges against him, his spirit-filled, faith-based, calm and forgiving death contrasts with the attackers, who are presented as a mob.

Stephen's calmness in death recalls Luke's description of Jesus' prayer as he dies that his spirit be received and his oppressors forgiven (Luke 23:34, 46). The first of the martyrs, Stephen demonstrates that we are called to live and die in the way that Jesus lived and died. From this story comes our confidence that God remains with us when we are persecuted, even when a mob demands death.

Observe that in 7:56, as the mob approaches, Stephen sees the Son of Man at the right hand of God. This parallels Jesus' comment to the council of elders in Luke 22:69. Both quotes refer to Daniel 7:13-14, where the Son of Man is at the hand of God. It is likely that the Jewish leaders saw this as blasphemy, while the Christians read this same passage as evidence that Jesus was indeed the anointed one. However, as we read to the end of the story, we see that Stephen's death ends the Christian mission in Jerusalem. Although the apostles remain, the resulting persecution scatters the church "throughout the countryside of Judea and Samaria" (Acts 8:1b). Saul, who is introduced here and leads the persecution, later will be Christianity's greatest apologist; yet he will not do his work here in Jerusalem but throughout the Hellenistic, Greek-speaking world.

Why is the martyrdom of Stephen, or of any believer, good news? There are many answers to this question; this study focuses on the relationship of different ethnic and cultural heritages with our faith. Notice how Stephen relies on the power of the Holy Spirit. Following Jesus' death, the disciples insist that Judas be replaced by someone who was part of Jesus' earthly journey; Peter preaches first to Aramaic-speaking Palestinian Jews, that is, people like himself.

Stephen, Hellenistic rather than Palestinian, newly converted rather than a long-time follower, and yet so clearly filled with the spirit, represents the first widening of the Christian vision. This is the beginning of the expanding circle of those who can hear the good news, who can live the life of Jesus. The Holy Spirit is already overflowing the boundaries we imagine. The story will continue as the Christians begin to embrace those God-fearers who have never been Jewish, and then the pagan community who never knew the God of Israel.

The test of who can know and be saved by Christ's message is changing. The Pentecost story breaks the barrier of language. Stephen breaks the barrier of culture. Paul will insist on breaking the barrier of law. The test of a believer will be the presence of the spirit rather than the connection to Jewish ethnic heritage.

> Then afterward
>> I will pour out my spirit on all flesh;
>> your sons and your daughters shall prophesy,

your old men shall dream dreams,
and your young men shall see visions.
Even on the male and female slaves,
in those days, I will pour out my spirit. (Joel 2:28)

In Acts 2:17, this passage from Joel is edited, changing "Then afterward" to "In the last days." Throughout Acts, we will find that the spirit is poured out on all flesh—regardless of race, class, or gender. It is in this widespread activity of the spirit that we have come to know and understand that the last days are here, and that they began with the resurrection of Jesus Christ.

Discussion Questions

1. From whose point of view is the story of Stephen written?
2. What is the good news from that point of view?
3. Who are the other characters of the story?
4. How might the story be different if they had written it?

As the discussion winds down, remind participants of the next week's reading, and close the session with prayer.

Closing Concerns and Prayer

LEADER: Let us pray:
ALL: Creator God, we thank you for the gift of being made in your image. We thank you for the way the diversity of the world reflects you. Teach us to always be widening our circle, sharing our hearts and our minds, teach us to trust the way the spirit moves us, and move others, toward you. Amen.

SESSION THREE:
EXODUS FROM A CANAANITE PERSPECTIVE: LOOKING FROM THE UNDERSIDE

Before the Session

Invite participants to read the excerpt from Robert Warrior's essay "Canaanites, Cowboys, and Indians" in Appendix 1.

Leader Preparation

- Set up the room if it does not remain set up from week to week.
- Assign someone to read the scripture during worship; mark Exodus 34:10-27 in the Bible.
- Select a hymn or music for the worship time.

Suggested Outline for Session Three

1. Opening worship (10 minutes)
2. Setting the tone: ground rules (5 minutes)
3. Finding perspective (25 minutes)
4. Considering scripture: Exodus (60 minutes)
5. Closing concerns and prayer (5-10 minutes)

Details of Session Three

Worship

LEADER:The Lord be with you
PEOPLE: and also with you
LEADER: Let us pray.
We gather together, Lord, to share your word with one another.
Guide us in our reading, in our studying, in our sharing, and guide
us, dear God, in our listening to each other, and to you.Teach us to
hear your word, and to live your word, with all our hearts, with all
our souls, with all our minds.Amen.

Scripture: Exodus 34:10–27

LEADER:Tell us what are you most proud of from your ethnic,
racial, or cultural heritage?

[allow sufficient time for sharing]

Singing: Choose a song from a people who have a history of suffering that is familiar to your group. If you do not have a song leader
in the study, consider playing a CD. Some suggestions include:

Signs of Endings All Around Us (WLP 721)
Carmina, Pueblo de Dios (WLP 739)
Wade in the Water (WLP 740)
Many and Great, O God, Are Thy Works (H1982 385)

Closing Prayer: ALL: O God, who created all peoples in your
image, we thank you for the wonderful diversity of races and cultures in this world. Enrich our lives by ever-widening circles of
fellowship, and show us your presence in those who differ most
from us, until our knowledge of your love is made perfect in our
love for all your children, through Jesus Christ our Lord. Amen.
(BCP, p. 840)

Setting the Tone

Review the ground rules again (this is especially important if the participants change from week to week).

Today our focus is on listening to the voices from the underside of the Exodus story, the underside of history, if you will. This is difficult at first, which is why we need to be careful in listening to each other, resisting the temptation to engage in arguments about interpretation.

The ground rule to pay special attention to today is: *We will practice dialogue, rather than debate*: we are not looking for one right answer. We will listen more and explain less. We will look for places of agreement. We will concentrate on feelings. Dialogue allows room for silence, and individuals may always choose to pass.

Finding Perspective

The saying goes: "The road to hell is paved with good intentions." While we often question our intentions and those of others—and all too often are quick to judge others'—lots of pain and suffering is caused not by bad intentions but by the impact of good ones. This exercise tries to get at the difference between "intent" and "impact" and invites the participants to think about and eventually take responsibility for the impact of well-intended words and actions.

Ask the participants if anyone remembers a situation, an incident when he or she was hurt by something that someone said or did, even though they knew the speaker meant well.

Ask for volunteers to share. Not everyone might be comfortable doing so.

Some examples:

1. A mother of two stepsons has another baby with the boys' father. His mother-in-law says: how wonderful! Now you are a real mother.
2. A parishioner of a predominantly white parish tells a newcomer: great to have you! We're always happy to welcome new people of color to the church. It helps our diversity.

3. A person using a wheelchair is slowly moving up the ramp to church. Another congregant runs up and pushes her to the door and into the church.

Discussion Questions

1. What is the good intention?
2. What is assumed?
3. What about it is potentially hurtful?
4. How does it feel to learn that my well-intended action was hurtful?
5. How could the situation be changed?

Considering Scripture, Exodus 15:1-21

Imagine you were a member of a Canaanite community. Some of you are working under the rule of a king who requires heavy taxes. Some of you are working the land of your ancestors. You have lived here as long as your family can remember.

Discussion Questions

1. Hearing this victory song of another people anew, what are you aware of?
2. What are your feelings? Your thoughts?
3. What parallels do you see to the history of this country?

At this point, the leader should be ready to summarize Robert Warrior's essay if participants have not read it and invite discussion. What issues does Warrior raise about the use of biblical texts? How does hearing the biblical story from the perspective of the Caananites change its impact? What are other examples you can suggest about the impact of culture on how we read biblical texts? Here the leader may encourage the group to look at other examples of the relationship between culture and interpretation of the Bible.

Background

Depending on time, it might be helpful to explore how the present
history of the biblical editors shapes an understanding of the story. If
Exodus was written in the exilic or even early postexilic time, after
the people experienced dislocation again and when they were long-
ing for another divine revelation of liberation from a foreign empire
or a sequence of foreign empires, how do we understand the faith
claims of "our" God wiping "them" out? What does this mean for relationships between people of different faiths? Theological questions
of exclusivity, of competing religions, are likely to arise and need to
be addressed here. Such questions are an opportunity for the leader
to engage participants on their views of other faith communities.

A Brief History of Interpretation

The story of the Exodus has been told and retold through the ages.
In Judaism, it has become the focal point of the annual observation
of the festival of Passover, when the story is reenacted in ritual. In
Christian traditions, the Exodus has figured prominently, from por-
traying Jesus as the new Moses to interweaving the Passover with
the Passion Narrative to various Christian communities who, for better or for worse, identified themselves as the people of the Exodus.
New England Puritans arriving in the Americas thought of themselves as the Israelites and the British as the Egyptians. Enslaved
women and men in the antebellum South called Harriet Tubman a
black Moses. Boer Nationalists in South Africa identified themselves
with the Israelites and considered the British the Egyptians. The War-
saw uprising in the Jewish ghetto also took the Exodus as a model.
Questions of "who's really who" abound. What happens when a dom-
inant group identifies itself as the chosen ones? What happens when
an oppressed group becomes the oppressor?

    In recent years, Latin American liberation theologies and black
theology have been the most prominent in identifying with the
Israelites of the Exodus. Both poor peasants and enslaved people of
African descent have found empowerment in the story. Critiques

have come from womanist theologians (see Williams's *Sisters in the Wilderness*), and even more so from First Nation peoples in the Americas (see Warrior's Native American perspective as an example).

So while we all identify with various characters and groups in the biblical text(s), it is important to differentiate between the varying perspectives in order not to use analogies in facile ways. So who are we really?

[If time permits, it might be helpful in contrast to make lists of qualities and actions of the various groups throughout the biblical story itself, and put them up on the walls around the room for further reference.]

Discussion Questions

Ask the participants to reflect on what it feels like to read and hear the Exodus story from the perspective of the Canaanites? What good news/life-giving message (if any) can they take away from this session?

Closing Concerns and Prayer
(from A New Zealand Prayer Book, *p. 637)*

LEADER: Let us pray together:
ALL: Universal and unchanging God, we are one, unalterably one, with all the human race. Grant that we who share Christ's blood may, through your unifying Spirit, break down the walls that divide us. Amen.

SESSION FOUR:
DIVERSITY:
WHO ARE THE PAGANS?

Before the Session

- Participants should read Acts 15.
- Review the previous session. You will be inviting reflections people have had from that session. Are there hot topics you need to be ready to discuss?
- Mark the scripture: Amos 9:11-12 and choose a hymn or set up a CD player for music.
- Assign participants readings for the worship time before the session begins.
- You will need a narrator, a Pharisee, someone to play Peter, and someone else to read James. Make copies of the readers' theater for each of the readers.
- The worship leader needs to be able to name something he or she is proud of about his or her own racial, cultural, or ethnic heritage.
- You will need five or six folding chairs for the FINDING PERSPECTIVE activity. It is best if one chair is a different color or style than the others.

Suggested Outline for Session Four

1. Opening worship (20 minutes)
2. Setting the tone: feelings from last time, ground rules (15 minutes)
3. Finding perspective (15 minutes)
4. Considering scripture: Acts 15:1-21 (60 minutes)
5. Closing concerns and prayer (10 minutes)

Details of Session Four

Worship

LEADER: The Lord be with you
PEOPLE: and also with you
LEADER: Let us pray.
We gather together, Lord, to share your word with one another. Guide us in our reading, in our studying, in our sharing, and guide us, dear God, in our listening to each other, and to you. Teach us to hear your word, and to live your word, with all our hearts, with all our souls, with all our minds. Amen.

Scripture: Amos 9:11-12

LEADER: Remember when you first noticed that there were different racial, ethnic, and cultural heritages. Did you notice different treatment based on these differences?
[This may be difficult for some. Please be patient and remember the permission to pass.]

Singing: Chose a song about the being raised up that is familiar to your group. If you do not have a song leader in the study, consider playing a CD.

I Will Raise You Up on Eagle's Wings (WLP 810)
We Shall Overcome (LEVAS 227)
Blessed Assurance (LEVAS 184)
Sekai no tomo to te otsunagi (WLP 793)

Closing Prayer: ALL: O God, who created all peoples in your image, we thank you for the wonderful diversity of races and cultures in this world. Enrich our lives by ever-widening circles of fellowship, and show us your presence in those who differ most from us, until our knowledge of your love is made perfect in our love for all your children, through Jesus Christ our Lord. Amen. (BCP, p. 840)

Setting the Tone

Remind the group of the ground rules and ask if they are helping. Consider adding additional rules if necessary. Ask how people feel about the previous week's study. Allow time for participants to name their concerns, and then ask again if others have different concerns. Today's study continues along a similar track, so the participants will be discussing the same issues.

Finding Perspective

Use these or similar words to introduce this session's activity: Sometimes we have power that we don't recognize. Sometimes we wish we had more power. This exercise looks at who has power in the abstract. Remember that power is not always a bad thing: the power to make things happen can be good.

Who Has the Power?

Provide five or six folding chairs that no one is sitting on. Set up the chairs in a format one might see at a meeting. Ask the group to observe the chairs and to discuss where the power is sitting in the setup. Then ask someone else to set up the chairs in a different format, and again ask where the power resides in the new format. Continue to invite participants to try various ways of setting up the chairs until the energy dies down or the concept seems exhausted.
Possible chair setups for the discussion include:

One chair faces the other four or five, which are in a row.
The chairs are evenly distributed in a circle, but one is a different color from the others.

The chairs are in an uneven oval, with one having more space around it than the others.

The chairs all face in the same direction, first a row of one, then two, then three chairs.

After the group has finished arranging the chairs, engage participants in a discussion about the setups using the questions listed below.

Discussion Questions

1. How does it feel to imagine power in different chairs?
2. How is power used well in your parish?

Considering Scripture, Acts 15:1-21

Today we turn to the story of the council at Jerusalem. Read the story today with an eye toward how it would feel to be a Gentile convert to Christianity.

An Introduction to the Characters

All of the characters in today's text are Jewish Christians. Peter and James are Palestinian Jews, speakers of Aramaic. Jerusalem is James's home, Peter is returning to his native land. In Acts, they are grouped with those called Hebrews. Palestinian Jews lived out a temple-focused faith that required purity only during holidays and when worshiping at the temple.

Paul, whose words are not recorded in this meeting, is a Pharisee. Although there was a sect called Pharisees during Jesus' time, this group grew in importance after the destruction of the temple. Pharisees promoted personal purity as a way of living out Judaism in their homes and neighborhoods. The Pharisees speaking at the council are mostly likely Palestinian, and thus heavily focused on food laws—including the rule of eating only with others who are following these laws. Hellenists, Jews of the Diaspora who followed the Pharisees, were more likely to focus on the sexual purity laws, since getting foods that were handled according to the strict customs of Palestine was almost impossible. Outside Palestine, it would be impossible to know if the food purchased had been offered to one of the many gods of the Roman Empire; in addition, it was unlikely that the appropriate tithes had been paid.

Not present, but under discussion, are the Gentiles who have converted to Christianity. Some of the converts have been described as God-fearers. These are Greek-speaking people who may or may not follow other Roman religions, and who attend synagogue worship with Jewish friends. They may be believers in the one God, but they are not circumcised and therefore are not converts to Judaism. Whatever they believed, God-fearers were Gentiles in the eyes of the Jews. As the text of Acts progresses, we find preaching outside the synagogue and Gentiles converting to the Christian faith. "Gentile" is a broad term, covering everyone who is not Jewish. Most of those who lived in the Roman Empire were Gentiles. Common practices in the variety of religions of the Roman Empire included offerings of gifts of meat and grains to the gods, festivals honoring the gods, and ritual sexual practices. Judaism and Christianity were distinctive in their requirement that a believer stick to one religion; it was not uncommon for Gentiles to be part of more than one sect.

Ask those assigned to read the scripture passage below (Acts 15:1–21) to the group.

NARRATOR: Then certain individuals came down from Judea and were teaching the brothers,

PHARISEE: "Unless you are circumcised according to the custom of Moses, you cannot be saved."

NARRATOR: And after Paul and Barnabas had no small dissension and debate with them, Paul and Barnabas and some of the others were appointed to go up to Jerusalem to discuss this question with the apostles and the elders. So they were sent on their way by the church, and as they passed through both Phoenicia and Samaria, they reported the conversion of the Gentiles, and brought great joy to all the believers.

PETER: When they came to Jerusalem, they were welcomed by the church and the apostles and the elders, and they reported all that God had done with them. But some believers who belonged to the sect of the Pharisees stood up and said,

PHARISEE: "It is necessary for them to be circumcised and ordered to keep the law of Moses."

NARRATOR: The apostles and the elders met together to consider this matter. After there had been much debate, Peter stood up and said to them,

PETER: "My brothers, you know that in the early days God made a choice among you, that I should be the one through whom the Gentiles would hear the message of the good news and become believers. And God, who knows the human heart, testified to them by giving them the Holy Spirit, just as he did to us; and in cleansing their hearts by faith he has made no distinction between them and us. Now therefore why are you putting God to the test by placing on the neck of the disciples a yoke that neither our ancestors nor we have been able to bear? On the contrary, we believe that we will be saved through the grace of the Lord Jesus, just as they will."

NARRATOR: The whole assembly kept silence, and listened to Barnabas and Paul as they told of all the signs and wonders that God had done through them among the Gentiles. After they finished speaking, James replied,

JAMES: "My brothers, listen to me. Simeon has related how God first looked favorably on the Gentiles, to take from among them a people for his name. This agrees with the words of the prophets, as it is written,

NARRATOR: (based on Amos 9:11-12) 'After this I will return, and I will rebuild the dwelling of David, which has fallen; from its ruins I will rebuild it, and I will set it up, so that all other peoples may seek the Lord—even all the Gentiles over whom my name has been called. Thus says the LORD, who has been making these things known from long ago.'

JAMES: "Therefore I have reached the decision that we should not trouble those Gentiles who are turning to God, but we should write to them to abstain only from things polluted by idols and from fornication and from whatever has been strangled and from blood. For in every city, for generations past, Moses has had those who proclaim him, for he has been read aloud every sabbath in the synagogues."

Discussion Questions

1. What jumps out at you from the text?
2. What is going on? What is the point of including this story in the text?
3. Who are the characters? Whose role is it easiest for you to identify with?

Commentary on Acts 15:1–21 as Background

In chapter 14 of Acts, Paul and Barnabas have returned to Antioch, and so the opening lines of this text are about Palestinian Jewish Christians—followers of the Pharisees, traveling to Antioch to be sure everyone is converted properly. For the Pharisees, this is a specific requirement. Converts must not only be circumcised—they must agree to adhere to the purity laws around food, washing, sexuality, and much of daily life.

But Jews and Jewish Christians outside the sect of the Pharisees were not following the law of Moses to the extent that the Pharisees demanded. Before the destruction of the temple, it was common for Jews to follow the purity laws around holidays and when visiting the temple. While we know that Paul was a Pharisee before becoming a Christian, the implication from Luke is that most of those who followed Jesus were not, in fact, sticklers for the details of purity laws. What all Jews had in common was not how they followed purity laws, but the fact that they were circumcised.

What is important to Paul and Barnabas is not circumcision or other purity laws, but "all that God had done with them" (Acts 15:4). Peter adds to this his story of how "God, who knows the human heart, testified to them by giving them the Holy Spirit, just as he did to us" (Acts 15:8). The point the three are making is that the test for who qualifies for God's grace has changed. The Jewish people have not successfully kept the law, yet the Holy Spirit keeps acting in the community, and acting in Jew and Gentile alike.

In fact, Peter's reminder seems aimed as much at the Jews in the room as at the Gentiles throughout the empire: "we believe that we will be saved through the grace of the Lord Jesus, just as they will" (Acts 15:11). It is not through the law of Moses that the Jews will be saved, so we certainly do not need the Gentiles to turn first to that, Peter is saying. Only Jesus Christ is needed for salvation.

James seems to agree, quoting from Amos that the temple, which is fallen, will be rebuilt, and the Gentiles will call God by name. James cannot give up all of the law, however, and sets up a few restrictions on Gentile converts, relying on the fact that the law of Moses has always been read in the synagogues. In essence, "we've always done it this way"!

Perhaps most striking, however, is who is included in the "we" of this discussion. This meeting of Christians to decide what it means to be a Gentile follower of Christ includes only Jews. There are not any Gentile converts invited or attending. Barnabas may have been Greek, from Cyprus (Acts 4:36), but he is the son of a Levite—that is, the family of a temple priest. He is part of the Jewish leadership. Peter and James, followers of Jesus when he was alive, were Jews from rural Palestine. Each person involved in the discussion of "what to do" about the Gentile Christians are Jewish Christians.

In fact, despite the reports of the workings of the spirit through the Gentiles they meet, almost every character in the Acts of the Apostles is a Jewish Christian. Peter baptizes the first Gentile, Cornelius, in Acts 10, and he is described as a God-fearer, a follower of the God of Abraham, not circumcised, but certainly familiar with the law of Moses. Although no one stands up against Cornelius's baptism, he is not invited to the council at Jerusalem.

What does it mean to come to a compromise without having all the interested parties in the room? And, if we are reading the text from the perspective of the Gentiles, is there actually a compromise? When reading today's text, try to imagine it from the perspective of a man like Cornelius, full of the spirit, full of God, excited to have found true faith. Cornelius will hear the good news in the form of a letter sent from the council, reporting their verdict.

Discussion Questions

  1. What do you think it felt like for new Gentile converts to be asked to accept Jewish scripture as the basis of the decision on whether they had to be Jewish before being Christian?

2. Does it matter that no Gentiles seem to have been part of the discussion?
3. Why do you think the Gentile Christians stuck with the faith?
4. Who has the power in this story? Who is involved in the decisions?

On that day I will raise up the booth of David that is fallen,
and repair its breaches, and raise up its ruins,
and rebuild it as in the days of old;
in order that they may possess the remnant of Edom
    and all the nations who are called by my name,
    says the LORD who does this. (Amos 9:11-12)

After this I will return,
    and I will rebuild the dwelling of David, which has fallen;
    from its ruins I will rebuild it, and I will set it up,
so that all other peoples may seek the Lord—
    even all the Gentiles over whom my name has been called.
    Thus says the Lord, who has been making these things
      known from long ago. (Acts 15:16-18)

In the original text, the raising up of David's house is a description of a future event, likely a prediction of the Day of the Lord. James's phrase "after this" declares that the day of the Lord is here, the dwelling of David is now being restored. And so, in this Jerusalem meeting, the transition described in Amos has occurred. Now is the time that "other peoples," the remnant of Edom and indeed "all the nations," are called by God.

In fact, it could be argued that Acts 15:16-18 is actually the message for the Gentiles. The power of God's word, it seems, is greater than even James can comprehend. James continues in verse 20 to speak not to the Gentiles, but to the Jewish Christians who are his followers. Perhaps he fears that the Jewish Christians will lose their "single-minded loyalty to God" if the Gentiles around them are not following the basic rules (see also James 1:8). While the letter is to be sent to the Gentiles, James's spoken words are intended for the Jewish Christians in that room.

Notice as well the actual content of the letter. The decision reached in verses 19 and 20 is to write to the Gentiles. Read verse 29, closing the actual letter, where the rules are stated, along with the phrase "you will do well to avoid these things." James is sending suggestions for helpful behavior to the Gentiles, not a list of rules to be followed. Perhaps James understands that the leaders in the room are not guiding events: the guide is the Holy Spirit, out in the world.

Discussion Questions

What does it feel like to read the text from the perspective of the Gentile converts? Does it feel like there is good news in this text?

Closing Concerns and Prayer
(from Joel 2:28-29 and Amos 9:11-12)

LEADER: Let us pray together:

ALL: Pour out your spirit on our flesh, O LORD, pour out your spirit upon us. Fill us with your spirit, that we might prophesy, that we might dream dreams, that we might see visions of your glory. Return and rebuild your house among us, so that we all might seek you, and know you, and call out your name. Amen.

SESSION FIVE:
EXODUS FROM THE EGYPTIAN PERSPECTIVE: WHAT IS THE GOOD NEWS?

Before the Session

Invite participants to read in advance the excerpt from Laurel Dykstra's book, *Set Them Free:The Other Side of Exodus*, found in Appendix 2.

Leader Preparation

- Prepare the worship and classroom space if needed.
- Make copies of the privilege list in section 3 to give out to participants.
- Gather paper and pencils for participants to use.
- Assign reader(s) for worship and mark the passages in the Bible.
- Select music for the worship time.

Suggested Outline for Session Five

1. Opening worship (10 minutes)
2. Setting the tone: ground rules (5 minutes)
3. Finding perspective (25 minutes)

4. Considering scripture: Exodus (60 minutes)
5. Closing concerns and prayer (5-10 minutes)

Details of Session Five

Worship

LEADER: The Lord be with you
PEOPLE: and also with you
LEADER: Let us pray.
We gather together, Lord, to share your word with one another.
Guide us in our reading, in our studying, in our sharing, and guide
us, dear God, in our listening to each other, and to you. Teach us to
hear your word, and to live your word, with all our hearts, with all
our souls, with all our minds. Amen.

Scripture: Deuteronomy 23:7; Exodus 6:1-8

LEADER: When you were a child, what did adults around you tell
you about people of other racial, ethnic, and cultural heritages? Did
family, friends, coaches, ministers, teachers, etc. speak in one voice,
or were the messages different? What were the unspoken messages?
[Listen carefully to the nuances during this sharing.]

Singing: Choose a song of struggle that is familiar to your group.
If you do not have a song leader in the study, consider playing a CD.

Go Down, Moses (LEVAS 228)
We'll Understand It Better By and By (LEVAS 207)

Closing Prayer: ALL: O God, who created all peoples in your
image, we thank you for the wonderful diversity of races and cultures in this world. Enrich our lives by ever-widening circles of fellowship, and show us your presence in those who differ most from
us, until our knowledge of your love is made perfect in our love for
all your children, through Jesus Christ our Lord. Amen. (BCP, p. 840)

Setting the Tone

Review ground rules again. Ask participants to focus on the ground rule: *we are each responsible for ourselves.* Ask them what this guideline means to them now, in light of the group's exploration of power issues and intentions.

Finding Perspective

We're going to explore issues around "privilege" this week. Privileges are generally presumed to be earned. For example, we receive the privilege of driving when we earn the right by passing a driver's test. However, there are some privileges that are given to us simply because we are born with particular traits. These are not things that we asked for and, in many cases, we would give them up if we could. Still, society as a whole hands out some "unearned privileges."

Working individually, read the list of privileges below.[2] Circle the ones that are accorded to you most of the time, and check the ones that you are granted occasionally.

- I am rarely asked to speak for all the people of my racial group.
- If I ask to talk to the person in charge, I'm pretty sure he or she will be of my race.
- If I am pulled over while driving, it is probably not because of my race.
- I can do well in a challenging situation and not be called a credit to my race.
- I can be sure if I need medical or legal help that my race will not be a factor.
- I can be late to a meeting without having my lateness reflect my race.
- I can worry about and call attention to prejudice and racism without being seen as self-interested.

---

2. Adapted from Peggy McIntosh, "White Privilege: Unpacking the Invisible Knapsack," *Peace and Freedom* (July/August 1989): 10–12.

- I can turn on the television or read a newspaper or magazine and find images of people of my race widely represented.
- I can have an emotional reaction in the workplace without others presuming this is a trait of my gender.
- I can be turned down for a promotion and not wonder if it was because of my gender.
- I can receive a promotion and not wonder if my gender influenced the amount of the raise.
- I can presume that my decisions about raising a family will not make others presume natural career consequences.
- I can go out after dark in most places without friends and family worried that I am risk taker.
- I can call myself a feminist without being seen as self-interested.
- I don't have to ask for permission to take most religious holidays off from work.
- I can presume my religion will be accepted as normal and understandable in my child's school.
- People mostly won't presume that what I eat or wear is based on my religious faith.
- My boss and most leaders at my work are familiar with my religion.
- When leaders of my faith do inappropriate things, people rarely assume that I do the same.

When participants have finished their lists, break them into small groups of three to five people to compare their results with each other. Ask them to talk with each other about how it feels to have been given—or not given—these privileges. Ask them also to address how privilege affects our society in general and our churches in particular. When the groups are finished, gather everyone back into the large group and ask them to share how they felt while marking the privileges.

Discussion Questions

1. How did it feel to share the results with your small group?
2. Did you find any similarities or differences within your group?

Considering Scripture, Exodus 15:1-21

Ask the group to imagine that they are Egyptians listening to this victory song. Some of you were sympathetic to the plight of individual Hebrews, but most of you took advantage of them for several generations. How do you hear their victory song? How can there be good news for the privileged? Lead a group discussion using the following questions as discussion starters.

Discussion Questions

> 1. Hearing this victory song of another people anew, what are you aware of?
> 2. What are your feelings? Your thoughts?
> 3. What parallels do you see to the history of this country?

Outline options for the "Egyptians" or the "privileged" of today's world, first in general, then in particular for your group/parish. What is God saying to those who have privilege? At this point, it might be helpful to review Laurel Dykstra's insights. If there is time, pushing some of the points of "New Ways of Acting" is recommended.

Further Discussion

Invite the participants to reflect on where we go from here and what kind of support they will need in order to begin the complex work of change.

Closing Concerns and Prayer
(Collect for Social Justice, BCP, p. 260)

> LEADER: Let us pray together:
> ALL: Almighty God, who created all of us in your own image: Grant us grace fearlessly to contend against evil and make no peace with oppression; and, that we may reverently use our freedom, help us to employ it in the maintenance of justice in our communities and among the nations, to the glory of your holy Name; through Jesus Christ our Lord, who lives and reigns with you and the Holy Spirit, one God, now and for ever. Amen.

SESSION SIX:
JEWS IN ACTS:
A PERSPECTIVE OF
ROMAN RULE

Before the Session

- Participants should read Acts 14.
- Mark the scripture: Acts 5:34-39.
- Choose a hymn or music from a CD.
- Gather materials for the exercise, including pens and books.
- You will need ten dice for this session, along with a small table to roll the dice on.
- Select readers for worship and for the readers' theater in advance of the session. For the readers' theater you will need a narrator, a man, Paul, and two people to be the crowd.
- Make copies of the readers' theater for those who will be reading aloud.

Suggested Outline for Session Six

1. Worship (15 minutes)
2. Setting the tone (15 minutes)

3. Finding perspective (30 minutes)
4. Considering the text:Acts 14:8–28 (45 minutes)
5. Closing concerns and prayer (15 minutes)

Details of Session Six

Worship

LEADER:The Lord be with you
PEOPLE: and also with you
LEADER: Let us pray.

We gather together, Lord, to share your word with one another. Guide us in our reading, in our studying, in our sharing, and guide us, dear God, in our listening to each other, and to you.Teach us to hear your word, and to live your word, with all our hearts, with all our souls, with all our minds.Amen.

Scripture:Acts 5:34–39

LEADER: How has racism, prejudice, and discrimination affected your life? How does it affect your parish?

[Extend the sharing as necessary. We encourage you to take notes for follow-up.]

Singing: Choose a song about the new creation that is familiar to your group. If you do not have a song leader in the study, consider playing a CD.

Great Is Thy Faithfulness (LEVAS 189)
What Wondrous Love Is This (H1982 439)
I've Got Peace Like a River (LEVAS 201)
Siyahambah ekukhanyen' kwenkhus' (WLP 787)
Camino, Pueblo de Dios (WLP 739)
Morning Has Broken (H1982 8)
Heleluyan (WLP 783)

Closing Prayer: ALL: O God, who created all peoples in your image, we thank you for the wonderful diversity of races and cultures in this world. Enrich our lives by ever-widening circles of fellowship, and show us your presence in those who differ most from us, until our knowledge of your love is made perfect in our love for all your children, through Jesus Christ our Lord. Amen. (BCP, p. 840)

Setting the Tone

Look at the ground rules once again. Conduct a short discussion on *We will not blame or shame ourselves or others.* How can we talk about mistakes and wrongdoing without blame or shame? How does the Christian concept of forgiveness influence our discussions? What does this ground rule suggest if someone doesn't believe they've done anything wrong?

Consider also the guideline *We will appreciate how we are different.* How does this fit with the Christian concept that we are all one in Christ?

Finding Perspective

Choose five people from your group to play today's game. Explain that the first round is not the actual game, but rather a sample to get the hang of it. Ask the five people to stand around a small table in the center of the group, with the other study members watching.

Give each of the five people two dice. Explain that the goal of the game is to collect the largest number of dice. One volunteer at a time challenges whomever he or she chooses to a roll-off. The two challengers roll their dice, and the winner gets all the dice. In the case of a tie, roll again. Players may not hide the number of dice they have accumulated. Allow a few challenges until everyone sees that eventually, the person with the most dice cannot be beaten—he or she has a higher score because he or she *is* rolling the most dice. Stop the game once everyone can see the pattern.

Take back all ten dice. Using the same group or new volunteers, give the first player five dice. Give the second player two dice. One die remains for each of the last three players. Then invite them to begin with the same rules: they may challenge whomever they choose. Allow the game to proceed to its conclusion.

Ask for five more volunteers. This time give out one die to each of the first four players, and the six remaining dice to one player. Ask the group: what is going to happen this time?

Discussion Questions

1. What happens to the people with the fewest dice in a game like this?
2. If you have only one or two dice, whom do you choose to challenge?
3. How would this game be different if we were playing with money, or food that we need for dinner?
4. How did it feel to be a person with fewer dice than another player? The person with more dice than others?
5. Thinking outside the box, what are better options for the players with few dice?

Considering Scripture, Acts 14:8-28

This session is complicated by the way New Testament anti-Judaism and modern anti-Semitism are intertwined with the topic. Our goal with today's text is to relate to the text as if *we* were the Jews—as if we were prosecuting and persecuting believers of a faith related to our own, and yet not quite the same as our own. The point is to get a handle on what it means to be in the position to persecute others—not just based on religion, but based on our race, our class, our gender, our perceived lack of disability, etc. In writing Acts, Luke depicts the Jews as oppressors; we are looking for the good news when we read the story as if we were the Jews.

It should not be lost on us that Christians throughout the world have used scriptures like this one to scapegoat Jews universally as oppressors. It was the failure of the German economic system, combined with anti-Jewish scripture, that let many Christians throughout Germany to accept that someone had to be blamed, that those people were the Jews, that separating the Jews made them safer, and finally, that killing was an appropriate solution.

The scripture for today describes the Jews as oppressors and, therefore, is instructive to us about the ways in which we are oppressors. Embedded in the text is a call to oppressors to step aside and let God's power guide the way. Luke is telling oppressors (the Jews, in this case) to stop interfering with the crowds, to stop blocking access to God, to stop standing in the way of the work of the Holy Spirit. Who are the oppressors in our communities today? Most importantly, what are the ways in which we are the oppressors?

Oppression is more complicated than simply declaring that I have more power than you do. And the story presented here is more complicated than Luke has described. The reality, almost certainly, is that the Jews are described as oppressors in Luke's effort to look good to Theophilus, an affluent Greek convert. As in the gospels, where the Jews rather than the Romans are accused of killing Jesus, the way Luke has told the Christian story in Acts emphasizes the struggles with the Jews. We know that only Rome—not the Jews or any other subject nation—could carry out the death penalty. We know as well that the Jewish homeland was destroyed by Rome in 70 BCE, and that it was Rome, not Jerusalem, that created most Christian martyrs.

As such, we aim to read today's scripture looking for good news: What is God calling us, to the extent that we are oppressors, to do?

NARRATOR: In Lystra there was a man sitting who could not use his feet and had never walked, for he had been crippled from birth.

MAN: He listened to Paul as he was speaking.

NARRATOR: And Paul, looking at him intently and seeing that he had faith to be healed, said in a loud voice,

PAUL: "Stand upright on your feet."

MAN: And the man sprang up and began to walk.

CROWD 1: When the crowds saw what Paul had done, they shouted in the Lycaonian language,

CROWD 2: "The gods have come down to us in human form!"

CROWD 1: Barnabas they called Zeus, and Paul they called Hermes, because he was the chief speaker. The priest of Zeus, whose temple was just outside the city, brought oxen and garlands to the gates; he and the crowds wanted to offer sacrifice.

NARRATOR: When the apostles Barnabas and Paul heard of it, they tore their clothes and rushed out into the crowd, shouting,

PAUL: "Friends, why are you doing this? We are mortals just like you, and we bring you good news, that you should turn from these worthless things to the living God, who made the heaven and the earth and the sea and all that is in them. In past generations he allowed all the nations to follow their own ways; yet he has not left himself without a witness in doing good—giving you rains from heaven and fruitful seasons, and filling you with food and your hearts with joy."

NARRATOR: Even with these words, they scarcely restrained the crowds from offering sacrifice to them.

CROWD 2: But Jews came there from Antioch and Iconium and won over the crowds. Then they stoned Paul and dragged him out of the city, supposing that he was dead.

NARRATOR: But when the disciples surrounded him, he got up and went into the city.

PAUL: The next day he went on with Barnabas to Derbe.

NARRATOR: After they had proclaimed the good news to that city and had made many disciples, they returned to Lystra, then on to Iconium and Antioch. There they strengthened the souls of the disciples and encouraged them to continue in the faith, saying,

PAUL: "It is through many persecutions that we must enter the kingdom of God."

MAN: And after they had appointed elders for them in each church, with prayer and fasting they entrusted them to the Lord in whom they had come to believe.

CROWD 1: Then they passed through Pisidia and came to Pamphylia. When they had spoken the word in Perga, they went down to Attalia. From there they sailed back to Antioch, where they had been commended to the grace of God for the work that they had completed.

CROWD 2: When they arrived, they called the church together and related all that God had done with them, and how he had opened a door of faith for the Gentiles. And they stayed there with the disciples for some time.

Discussion Questions

1. What jumps out about this story?
2. What is happening in this story? What is Luke's trying to communicate in telling this story?
3. Who are the major characters? Which characters are easiest to identify with?

Commentary on Acts 14:8-28 as Background

Note that Paul has fled to this scene, leaving behind the synagogues of Iconium, where a divided community persecuted him. This text opens with Paul healing a lame man, in the Gentile world of Lystra, a parallel to Peter's healing of a lame man in the Jewish world of Jerusalem (Acts 3). While the lame man believes, the pagan audience is clearly confused by the healing. They react by worshiping Paul and Barnabas as gods, and even after Paul's repeated preaching to the contrary, they cannot be dissuaded. Paul's arguments are interesting, logically starting with the statement that he and Barnabas are human, like the crowd, but then proceeding with language from the Hebrew scriptures about God's creation of heaven and earth. The God of Israel, not Zeus or Hermes, has provided the rain, food, and joy.

While Paul has no power to change the hearts or minds of these ignorant pagans, the Jews from Iconium and Antioch are much more convincing. Led by Jews, the pagan crowds turn against Paul, stoning him and dragging him outside the city limits. Stoning, you will remember, is the punishment within Judaism for blasphemy. And yet, at least in the text of the story before us, there is no evidence that Paul preached anything other than the power of the God of Israel.

Why the Jews would incite the people of Lystra to violence is not clear, but this story fits the pattern that Luke presents throughout Acts. Successful missionary activity leads to opposition, usually by Jews. The opposition is followed by release and the expansion of the Christian church. We see here that Paul appears to be dead but is not. The message to the Christians seems to be that the persecution is what is making the church succeed and expand. What is the message, however, if we imagine ourselves to be the Jews in the story?

Teasing out the intricacies of the relationship of Jews to Jewish Christians in Acts requires that we also identify the Roman Empire as a player in the early church. At the time that Acts was written, the Jews, dispersed throughout the empire, likely felt their position was precarious. Roman armies in 70 CE had destroyed their homeland and temple and exiled their leaders. While Hellenistic Jews of the Diaspora were well integrated into Roman society, their identity was still linked to the faith of Jerusalem, now under direct Roman rule.

Modern readers are likely to imagine the Judaism we know today in this text: one of home worship, synagogue attendance, and a focus on ethical practices. However, this Judaism was just developing in 80 CE; Jewish leaders may not have been confident the faith could endure. Liturgy was the center of first-century Judaism—a liturgy carried out in the temple.

The destruction of Judaism's central icon was a major pressure. The pressure these Jews who were following a messiah introduced was probably a small annoyance. Just as Judaism was focusing on drawing up a new definition of what it means to be Jewish, this small group of Jews—the Christians—were blurring the line, changing the rules, integrating people without a connection to the Jewish heritage. Pharisaic Judaism was strengthening the ties between individual Jews: developing rituals and customs for the home, enforcing purity laws to keep the community connected to their faith, and developing stronger ties to one another. Building stronger internal ties within community creates a more clear-cut boundary separating the community from those on the outside.

The Christian Jews not only refused to focus on these rituals and customs, they also made a scene in public. Public preaching, prominent attacks against the local culture, and outright evangelism all called attention to Judaism. Look again at Acts 14:15-17. Paul's preaching sounds orthodox to modern Christians, but he is essentially telling the pagans their religion and their gods are ridiculous, and they should turn to the God the Jews worship, the God who created them. Pharisaic Judaism needs to shut down this disobedient Jewish sect for the safety and survival of their community. Paul and the Christian Jews repeatedly refuse to consider safety a goal. The Christians declare that it is "through many persecutions that we must enter the kingdom of God" (Acts 14:22).

This is the story of a persecuted community: the Jews of the Roman Empire, fighting among themselves about how best to live under that persecution. This story concludes, in Acts 21-28, with the Jews turning Paul over to the Roman authorities in their effort to prove that they are not connected to this conflict-creating Christian sect.

Discussion Questions

1. What was God calling the Jews to do in this story?
2. What is God calling us to do when we are fighting with others who are like us?
3. What is God calling us to do when we are afraid? Oppressed? Persecuted?

Closing the Study

For the past six sessions, we have delved into the foundational stories about making communities in the book of Exodus and in the Acts of the Apostles. We have listened and learned, struggled and rejoiced in new insights. We have begun to see familiar stories from new perspectives, perspectives that, depending on our social locations, do not always feel comfortable. Our commitment to the struggle for justice urges us to stay with this discomfort and let it motivate us to keep on keeping on in the work for change, even if the steps are tiny and the task feels overwhelming at times. We need to act as if our lives depended on this work, because they do. So if you take only one nugget from this experience, let it be one of asking the deeper questions of who is at the table, who is left out, who is there but rendered silent. In the name of the One who calls us to be justice makers. Amen.

Closing Prayer (BCP, p. 827)

LEADER: Let us pray
ALL: Grant, O God, that your Holy and life-giving Spirit may so move every human heart (and especially the hearts of people of this land), that barriers which divide us may crumble, suspicions disappear, and hatreds cease; that, our divisions being healed, we may live in justice and peace; through Jesus Christ our Lord. Amen.

APPENDIX 1

A Native American Perspective[3]

Most of the liberation theologies that have emerged in the last twenty years are preoccupied with the Exodus story, using it as the fundamental model for liberation. I believe that the story of the Exodus is an inappropriate way for Native Americans to think about liberation.

No doubt, the story is one that has inspired many people in many contexts to struggle against injustice. Israel, in the Exile, then Diaspora, would remember the story and be reminded of God's faithfulness. Enslaved African Americans, given Bibles to read by their masters and mistresses, would begin at the beginning of the book and find in the pages of the Pentateuch a god who was obviously on their side, even if that god was the god of their oppressors. People in Latin America base communities read the story and have been inspired to struggle against injustice. The Exodus, with its picture of a god who takes the side of the oppressed and the powerless, has been a beacon of hope for many in despair.

---

3. Excerpts from "A Native American Perspective: Canaanites, Cowboys, and Indians" by Robert Allen Warrior, reprinted in *Voices from the Margin: Interpreting the Bible in the Third World*, ed. R. S. Sugirtharajah (Maryknoll, NY: Orbis Books, 1991), pp. 288-92, 293-94.

God The Conqueror

Yet, the liberationist picture of Yahweh is not complete. A delivered people is not a free people, nor is it a nation. People who have survived the nightmare of subjugation dream of escape. Once the victims have been delivered, they seek a new dream, a new goal, usually a place of safety away from the oppressors, a place that can be defended against future subjugation. Israel's new dream became the land of Canaan. And Yahweh was still with them: Yahweh promised to go before the people and give them to Canaan, with its flowing milk and honey. The land, Yahweh decided, belonged to these former slaves from Egypt and Yahweh planned on giving it to them—using the same power used against the enslaving Egyptians to defeat the indigenous inhabitants of Canaan. Yahweh the deliverer became Yahweh the conqueror.

The obvious characters in the story for the Native Americans to identify with are the Canaanites, the people who already lived in the promised land. As a member of the Osage Nation of the American Indians who stands in solidarity with other tribal people around the world, I read the Exodus stories with Canaanite eyes. And, it is the Canaanite side of the story that has been overlooked by those seeking to articulate theologies of liberation. Especially ignored are those parts of the story that describe Yahweh's command to mercilessly annihilate the indigenous population.

To be sure, most scholars, of a variety of political and theological stripes, agree that the actual events of Israel's early history are much different than what was commanded in the narrative. The Canaanites were not systematically annihilated, nor were they completely driven from the land. In fact, they made up, to a large extent, the people of the new nation of Israel. Perhaps it was a process of gradual immigration of people from many places and religions who came together to form a new nation. Or maybe, as Norman Gottwald and others have argued, the peasants of Canaan revolted against their feudal masters, a revolt instigated and aided by a vanguard of escaped slaves from Egypt who believed in the liberating god, Yahweh. Whatever happened, scholars agree that the people of Canaan had a lot to do with it.

Nonetheless, scholarly agreement should not allow us to breathe a sigh of relief. For historical knowledge does not change the status of the indigenes in the *narrative* and the theology that grows out of it. The research of Old Testament scholars, however much it provides an answer to the historical question—the contribution of the indigenous people of Canaan to the formation and emergence of Israel as a nation—does not solve the narrative problem. People who read the narratives read them as they are, not as the scholars and experts *like* them to be read and interpreted. History is no longer with us. The narrative remains.

Though the Exodus and Conquest stories are familiar to most readers, I want to highlight some sections that are commonly ignored. The covenant begins when Yahweh comes to Abram saying, "Know of a surety that your descendents will be sojourners in a land that is not theirs, and they will be slaves there, and they will be oppressed for four hundred years; but I will bring judgment on the nation they serve and they shall come out" (Gen. 15:13, 14). Then, Yahweh adds: "To your descendents I will give this land, the land of the Kenites, the Kenizzites, the Kadmonites, the Hittites, the Perizzites, the Rephaim, the Amorites, the Canaanites, and the Jebusites" (15:18-21). The next important moment is the commissioning of Moses. Yahweh says to him, "I promise I will bring you out of the affliction of Egypt, to the land of the Canaanites, the Hittites, the Amorites, the Perizzites, the Hivites, and the Jebusites, a land flowing with milk and honey" (Exod. 3:17). The covenant, in other words, has two parts: deliverance and conquest.

After the people have escaped and are headed to the promised land, the covenant is made more complicated, but it still has two parts. If the delivered people remain faithful to Yahweh, they will be blessed in the land Yahweh will conquer for them (Exod. 20-30 and Deut. 7-10). The god who delivered Israel from slavery will lead the people into the land and keep them there as long as they live up to the terms of the covenant. "You shall not wrong a stranger or oppress him [*sic*], for you were strangers in the land of Egypt. You shall not afflict any widow or orphan. If you do afflict them, and they cry out to me, I will surely hear their cry; and my wrath will burn, and I will kill you with the sword, and your wives shall become widows and your children fatherless" (Exod. 22:21).

Whose Narrative?

Israel's reward for keeping Yahweh's commandments—for building a society where the evils done to them have no place—is the continuation of life in the land. But one of the most important of Yahweh's commands is the prohibition on social relations with Canaanites or participation in their religion. "I will deliver the inhabitants of the land into your hand, and you shall drive them out before you. You shall make no covenant with them or with their gods. They shall not dwell in your land, lest they make you sin against me; for if you serve their gods it will surely be a snare to you" (Exod. 23:31b–33).

In fact, the indigenes are to be destroyed:

> When the Lord your God brings you into the land which you are entering to take possession of it, and clears away many nations before you, the Hittites, the Girgashites, the Amorites, the Canaanites, the Perizzites, the Hivites, and the Jebusites, seven nations greater and mightier than yourselves, and when the Lord your God gives them over to you and you defeat them; then you must utterly destroy them; you shall make no covenant with them, and show no mercy to them. (Deut. 7:1, 2)

These words are spoken to the people of Israel as they are preparing to go into Canaan. The promises made to Abraham and Moses are ready to be fulfilled. All that remains for the people is to enter into the land and dispossess those who already live there.

Joshua gives an account of the conquest. After ten chapters of stories about Israel's successes and failures to obey Yahweh's commands, the writer states, "So Joshua defeated the whole land, the hill country and the Negeb and the lowland and the slopes, and all their kings, he left none remaining, but utterly destroyed all that breathed, as the Lord God of Israel commanded." In Judges, the writer disagrees with this account of what happened, but the Canaanites are held in no higher esteem. The angel of the Lord says, "I will not drive out [the indigenous people] before you; but they shall become adversaries to you, and their gods shall be a snare to you."

Thus, the narrative tells us that the Canaanites have status only
as people Yahweh removed from the land in order to bring the chosen people in. They are not to be trusted, nor are they allowed to
enter into social relationships with the people of Israel. They are
wicked, and their religion is to be avoided at all costs. The laws put
forth regarding strangers and sojourners may have stopped the people of Yahweh from wanton oppression, but presumably only after
the land was safely in the hand of Israel. The covenant of Yahweh
depends on this.

The Exodus narrative is where discussion about Christian
involvement in Native American activism must begin. It is these stories of deliverance and conquest that are ready to be picked up and
believed by anyone wondering what to do about the people who
already live in their promised land. They provide an example of what
can happen when powerless people come into power. Historical
scholarship may tell a different story; but even if the annihilation did
not take place, the narratives tell what happened to those indigenous people who put their hope and faith in ideas and gods that
were foreign to their culture. The Canaanites trusted in the god of
outsiders and their story of oppression and exploitation was lost.
Interreligious praxis became betrayal and the surviving narrative
tells us nothing about it. . . .

Is There a Spirit?

What is to be done? First, the Canaanites should be at the center of
Christian theological reflection and political action. They are the last
ignored voice in the text, except perhaps for the land itself. The conquest stories, with all their violence and injustice, must be taken
seriously by those who believe in the god of the Old Testament.
Commentaries and critical works rarely mention these texts. When
they do, they express little concern for the status of the indigenes
and their rights as human beings and as nations. The same blindness
is evident in theologies that use the Exodus motif as their basis for
political action. The leading into the land becomes just one more
redemptive moment rather than a violation of innocent peoples'
rights to land and self-determination.

Keeping the Canaanites at the center makes it more likely that those who read the Bible will read *all* of it, not just the part that inspires and justified them. And should anyone be surprised by the brutality, the terror of these texts? It was, after all, a Jewish victim of the Holocaust, Walter Benjamin, who said, "There is no document of civilization which is not at the same time a document of barbarism." People whose theology involves the Bible need to take this insight seriously. It is those who know these texts who must speak the truth about what they contain. It is to those who believe in these texts that the barbarism belongs. It is those who act on the basis of these texts who must take responsibility for the terror and violence they can and have engendered. . . .

No matter what we do, the conquest narratives will remain. As long as people believe in Yahweh of deliverance, the world will not be safe from Yahweh the conqueror. But perhaps, if they are true to their struggle, people will be able to achieve what Yahweh's chosen people in the past have not: a society of people delivered from oppression who are not so afraid of becoming victims again that they become oppressors themselves, a society where the original inhabitants can become something other than subjects to be converted to a better way of life or adversaries who provide cannon fodder for a nation's militaristic pride.

With what voice will we, the Canaanites of the world, say, "Let my people go and leave my people alone?" And, with what ears will followers of alien gods who have wooed us (Christians, Jews, Marxists, capitalists), listen to us? The indigenous people of this hemisphere have endured a subjugation now 100 years longer than the sojourn of Israel in Egypt. Is there a god, a spirit, who will hear us and stand with us in the Amazon, Osage County, and Wounded Knee? Is there a god, a spirit, able to move among the pain and anger of Nablus, Gaza, and Soweto? Perhaps. But we, the wretched of the earth, may be well advised this time not to listen to outsiders with their promises of liberation and deliverance. We will perhaps do better to look elsewhere for our vision of justice, peace, and political sanity—a vision through which we escape not only our oppressors, but our oppression as well. Maybe, for once, we will have to listen to ourselves, leaving the gods of this continent's real strangers to do battle among themselves.

APPENDIX 2

Reading Exodus in the First World[4]

In reading Guider, Williams, Warrior and other writers like them, it became clear to me that if I was going to learn anything new or authentic about Exodus, it would be by attending to my own situation and reading from the perspective of those in the text whom I most resemble.

It seems to be inadequate simply to transpose this theology, wrung from suffering into the "First World." It is inadequate because we of the first world live in a different socio-economic context and liberation theology rightly insists that theology must be contextual."[5]

Liberation theologian Jon Sobrino says, "the fundamental division in humankind is that between life and death, between those who die because of oppression and those who live because of it."

---

4. Excerpts from *Set Them Free: The Other Side of Exodus* by Laurel A. Dykstra (Maryknoll, New York: Orbis Books, 2002).
5. Norbert Greinacher, "Liberation Theology in the 'First World'?" in *Option for the Poor: Challenge to the Rich Countries*, ed. Leonardo Boff and Virgil Elizondo (Edinburgh: T&T Clark, 1986), p. 81.

When put in these stark terms, it is clear to me that as a white, first-world, North American, able-bodied, Protestant Christian, I am among those who live because of oppression. My access to food, clothing, shelter, education, and employment, all of which I have expended some effort for, is predicated upon violent systems of extraction and exploitation. The simple luxuries of my daily living—a computer, a sweatshirt, fresh fruit—are available to me *because* twelve-year-olds work in free-trade-zone factories, garment workers earn starvation wages, and agricultural workers are exposed to pesticides. In Exodus it is the Israelites who die because of oppression and the Egyptians who live because of it. Following the examples of Guider, Williams, and Warrior, if I am to bring my own experience to Exodus, then I must identify with the Egyptians, the villains of the story. I must explore their traits and qualities.

Perhaps some readers will object that I am identifying only with my privilege. It is true that I am a low-income queer woman, and a single parent in a culture that punishes poverty, difference, femaleness, I am among those who die because of oppression. I am no different from the young women who were massacred at the Polytechnique in Montreal; in 1989 I also was an undergraduate science student at a Canadian university. I am no different from Rebecca Wright, Brandon Teena, or Matthew Shepard, who were murdered because they were lesbian, transgender, gay. In my home and on the streets, I am no different from the women, children, gays, lesbian, bisexuals, and transgender people who are beaten, raped, stabbed, shot, and killed in escalating numbers every day. Like everyone I know, I have experiences of privilege and experiences of oppression; but "privilege on one power axis does not negate oppression on another."

In the past twenty years postmodern thinkers, particularly women of color, like Audre Lord and Gloria Anzaldua, have challenged the notion of a single unified self. They affirm that each person has multiple identities, we live in a pluralistic world, and texts may have more than one truth. The acceptance of these insights has made biblical readings from marginal perspectives, like those of Guider, Williams, and Warrior, possible. Where once texts were thought to have a single, fixed, and known meaning, now there is a possibility for a rich exchange of perspectives.

With this opening to new voices and perspectives has come a disturbing backlash to which white academics are particularly prone. The argument goes something like this: since concepts such as truth, meaning, or justice are not grounded in any reality that applies across culture and language, any move to evaluate a reading in terms of accuracy, rigor, or liberative potential is an illegitimate attempt to assert a new universalism or impose some false authority. The insidious result is that nothing changes; with their sheer volume and familiarity, the old, white patriarchal readings maintain their place of privilege by default. I think of this phenomenon as post-modern paralysis.

> When I think no thing is like any other thing
> I come speechless, cold, my body turns silver
> and water runs off me. There I am
> ten feet from myself, possessor of nothing,
> uncomprehending of even the smallest piece of dust.
> —James Tate

Reading for Our Lives

I believe that each of us, in the Exodus story, is *both* Israel and Egypt. We are called to go out from the land of bondage *and* let the oppressed go free. Thus, for the remainder of this book I will focus on the similarities between Egyptians in Exodus and privileged first-world Christians. This is not an exercise in white liberal guilt; it is an accurate reflection of our situation. I identify with our privilege because, in a global context it is immense. Further, as a starting point for biblical reflection, to clearly identify our own context is a require-ment of good scholarship. Finally, I identify with Egypt because for first-world Christians it is the best possible reading. It reflects our sit-uation, accounts for power dynamics, and may even help us to par-ticipate in the work of justice.

For the duration of this book, I will maintain the assumption that first-world readers resemble the Egyptians, as an exercise in what Mary Ann Tolbert calls "protesting our privilege." This means not behaving as if our position on the high side of the material divide and the fact that, however comfortable, it is neither just nor deserved. I invite the reader to join with me in this challenging exploration of Exodus. Looking at how we resemble the villains in this story may not be comfortable or flattering; it may teach us things about ourselves that we would rather not know. My intention is not to blame to create bad feelings. It is to unmask destructive systems in which we participate, so that we can begin to dismantle the culture of domination in which we live. Knowing what we do, what is destructive and what is constructive, can help us to change the patterns of our behavior so that despite privilege we may be a part of God's liberation project.

Setting the People Free: A Commissioning

This book was written out of loyalty to white middle-income church people, the people who, most unintentionally, taught me to love the Bible. I am angry that these who are my people—at least as much as the street folks and addicts, prostitutes, and mentally ill who now occupy my days—hear biblical readings that are almost exclusively personal. These personal readings "turn the Bible's religious passion for social justice into a teaching about individual salvation which has the net effect of rationalizing and perpetuating social inequity."[6] In the case of Exodus, such personalized readings ask middle-class people, "What keeps you from being liberated?" Readings of Exodus that focus on how the affluent are oppressed fail. They fail the poor by making their suffering invisible, they fail the text by making its political, community message psychological and personal, and they fail the rich by fearing to challenge them to the hard change and repentance that is liberation. My goal in writing is that people of privilege who identify as Christian will come to take the Bible's passion for justice seriously in their own lives and become involved in the work of justice. My hope is that my people will come out of empire.

A fundamental premise of this book is that first-world Christians, reading together, can use the sacred gift of our tradition to

---

6. Tom Faw Driver, *Christ in a Changing World: Toward an Ethical Christology* (New York: Crossroad, 1981), 4.

grapple with and live out our own stories in the empire of global capitalism. The Bible is a gift of our ancestors born of the love of God and struggle to do right in the world. In our modern self-absorption and shortsightedness, we have lost all reverence for the wisdom of our ancestors. It is difficult for modern people, and especially middle-class white people, to admit that anybody knows better than us, let alone people who lived thousands of years ago. But Exodus asks questions that are relevant beyond the book's ancient African and Near Eastern contexts.

- Who controls the lands?
- Does the earth have its own integrity?
- Do poor people matter?
- Does power automatically deserve allegiance?
- How do you know if the law is right?
- Where do good things/good life come from?
- What is God like?
- Is empire the only way to live?
- What determines membership in a group?
- What are the characteristics of empire?

These questions are as relevant to those of us living under global capitalism today as they were thousands of years ago. In the previous chapters we explored some of these questions. Before we look at the task of leaving empire, let us briefly revisit some of the answers we have gleaned from Exodus.

A Review

The core argument of this book is that first-world Christians have more in common with Egypt than with Israel in Exodus, and that this is a hermeneutical key that can unlock both Exodus and our own lives. Through the characters of the two pharaohs and the functioning of Egypt, Exodus presents us with a century-old portrait of empire from the perspective of the oppressed. From our context of today's global economy we can see how empire has changed over time. We can look at the qualities of empire: exploitation, slavery, genocide, deceit, and the various ways that people of privilege participate and collude in them. Looking specifically at the land of Egypt in Exodus allows us to focus on environmental/ecological issues in our own time, particularly issues of women and the environment and the connections between modern corporate exploitation of the natural world and of other humans.

Exodus is pervasively and disturbingly violent, with the pharaohs and YHWH being the most violent actors. Honestly addressing this violence in scripture can help us to address the structural violence in our own culture and to ask who carries it out and against whom. Exploring the violence in Exodus causes us to look at the connections and differences between violent stories and violent actions. First-world Christians can see the stories of Egypt in Exodus as a means of exploring our own participation in the modern empire of global capitalism. Knowing and recognizing our patterns of addiction to empire is the first step in breaking them.

In Exodus, Shiphrah and Puah and Pharaoh's daughter are Egyptian women from different levels of privilege who defy the law and act courageously with and on behalf of the oppressed. There are hints and indicators that other Egyptians too were part of the Exodus project. The great gift of these stories is that the Israelite narrators of the Exodus considered Egyptians to be capable of such acts of solidarity. This is an enormous vote of confidence for those of us who seek to live counter to empire today. However, the stories also show some of the complexities and ambiguities of trying to act and live in solidarity, the pitfalls of trying to cross, not from Egypt to Canaan, but simply from power to less power. According to Gregory Baum, a Canadian theologian, Israel's dissent and mutiny in the wilderness attest to the ambiguity of the people's commitment to liberation. How much more ambiguous is the commitment of the privileged to liberation when in material terms we stand to lose?

Reading the Bible as we have in this book, as sacred story, can be tremendously valuable for people of privilege. Exodus is neither a history text nor a personal instruction book for life. Using the tools of critical scholarship, we can bring our minds to scripture and understand how a passage's very specific context might be compared to our own. Grappling with the parts of the text that disturb us or [that are] at complete odds with our own values inoculates us against the dangerous phrase "the Bible says" as a hammer or a weapon. By placing our Egyptian reading of Exodus beside other liberation readings we open ourselves to critical evaluation from others seeking justice, and we are prevented from imagining that we have the one true interpretation. At the same time, being grounded in our own social and political context and being clear about our own assumptions and values provides a basis from which to evaluate our own and others' interpretations. Thus we can stand firm in our commitment to justice and need not fall into the fallacy of asserting that all interpretations are equally valid.

Where Do We Go from Here?

The Exodus authors had confidence that people of privilege could actively resist empire and be allies of the oppressed, but in the modern world of global capitalism this is a tremendous task. We are seeking in some real sense to leave behind everything we have known, for we have been raised and nurtured on empire. The challenge we face is compounded by the fact that we do not have the option of simple departure. We cannot, like Israel, go feral. There is no Promised Land lying empty and waiting for us; indeed there was not for Israel. Corporate globalization is such that the most remote enclaves and peoples are still touched by it. We must then resist empire while remaining somehow within it.

Empire surrounds us so completely that it is essentially invisible. Pop machines, skyscrapers, automobiles, television—the most ordinary stuff of our lives—is the effluvium of empire. We are continually plied with comfort and convenience that muffle any question or protest. But the fact that affluent lives may still be filled with suffering and struggle can render privilege invisible to those who have it. Those of us who would resist empire are faced with a difficult task. To see the luxury that surrounds us as anything but right and normal puts us profoundly out of step with our peers. Questioning empire, let alone saying no to it, seems impossible, absurd. What empire offers us is fun, fast, and glitzy, but more than anything else, it is normal.

By contrast, resistance and the work of solidarity are sometimes low, boring, and inconvenient. Friends, family and the people we live with may not understand what we are trying to do. This can be lonely and alienating. It can be even more lonely when those whom we seek to join and support do not welcome us with open arms. When our intentions are good it can be hard to realize that the oppressed have every reason to mistrust us. Religion too can impede our task, for since the time of Constantine, the church has supported and modeled itself after empire. By all that empire has taught us to value, becoming allies of the oppressed is an exchange in which we stand to lose.

Corporate capitalism so pervades our lives and our planet that any resistance we offer seems terribly small. Success is one of the key elements of empire's mythology. For those of us raised on this myth it can be incredibly frustrating to feel that our efforts are futile or that we are constantly failing. When we cannot hope to win it is difficult for us to resist. Global capitalism is profoundly opposed to love of humanity, love of the earth, and love of God. A system based on domination cannot be fixed, but we can offer alternatives. Winning is not the overthrow of empire; it is any action that suggests that empire is not the only way.

We are faced with an enormous task, but this is the stuff that great stories are made of: leaving behind what has always represented security, starting out on a journey of discovery that will show us what lies behind the world we know. In order to survive in this new world we will need new ways of thinking and acting. In the introduction to this book, I laid out certain criteria for the evaluation of this reading of Exodus: dangerousness, subversiveness, insightfulness, usefulness, creativity, ferocity, rigor, honesty, joy, and faithfulness. In these last pages of this book I want to focus specifically on the criterion of usefulness. It is not enough that people read this book; it is my hope that through this reading people will come together to act for change. To do this we need to change the ways we think, and speak, and act.

In Closing

A list of precepts and prescriptions can seem vague or abstract, and these proposed ways of thinking and acting may be daunting, especially if they are new. Truly the call to live counter to the world around us carries rigorous demands, but the new life we are promised is exciting and joyful. In small ways all around the world there are individuals, organizations, and communities living out their resistance to empire, simply and creatively. Gandhi called these efforts "experiments in truth." As we undertake our own experiences, first-world Christians can be sustained and strengthened by stories; our biblical heritage.

The heritage of Exodus is a great and honest gift for privileged readers. Exodus does not diminish the seduction and the appeal of empire, nor does it pretend that salvation can be found there. By reading Exodus and identifying with the Egyptians we have faced hard truths about ourselves and the way we serve the empire of global capitalism. Like Egypt, we are complicit in oppression, slavery, and genocide. Facing these truths is the beginning of true conversion. First-world Christians live daily in the centers of global capitalism, but together with Shiprah and Puah and Pharaoh's daughter, with one another, and with whoever will have us as allies, we can come out of empire. "Exodus is the journey of the whole humanity and of creation toward the resurrection of all flesh and the renewal of heaven and earth."[7] Amen.

---

7. Leonardo Boff, quoted in Dan Cohn-Sherbrook, *Exodus: An Agenda for Jewish-Christian Dialogue* (London: Bellew, 1992), 77.

BIBLIOGRAPHY

Anti-Racism Committee of the Executive Council. *Seeing the Face of God in Each Other: A Manual for Anti-Racism Training and Action*. New York: The Episcopal Church Center, 2003.

Back, Les, and John Solomos, eds. *Theories of Race and Racism: A Reader*. London and New York: Routledge, 2000.

Childs, Brevard. *The Book of Exodus: A Critical Commentary*. Old Testament Library. Philadelphia: Westminster Press, 1974.

Cohn-Sherbrook, Dan. *Exodus: An Agenda for Jewish-Christian Dialogue*. London: Bellew, 1992.

Cone, James. *A Black Theology of Liberation*. Maryknoll, NY: Orbis Books, 1990.

———. *God of the Oppressed*. New York: Seabury, 1975.

Countryman, L. William. *Dirt, Greed & Sex: Sexual Ethics in the New Testament and Their Implications for Today*. Philadelphia: Fortress, 1988.

Croatto, J. Severino. *Exodus: A Hermeneutics of Freedom*. Maryknoll, NY: Orbis Books, 1981.

Delgado, Richard, and Jean Stefancic, eds. *Critical White Studies: Looking Behind the Mirror*. Philadelphia: Temple University Press, 1997.

Dykstra, Laurel A. *Set Them Free: The Other Side of Exodus*. Maryknoll, NY: Orbis Books, 2002.

Harvey, Jennifer, et al., eds. *Disrupting White Supremacy from Within: White People on What We Need to Do*. Cleveland, OH: Pilgrim Press, 2004.

Hobgood, Mary Elizabeth. *Dismantling Privilege: An Ethics of Accountability*. Cleveland, OH: Pilgrim Press, 2000.

McIntosh, Peggy. "White Privilege: Unpacking the Invisible Knapsack." *Peace and Freedom* (July/August 1989): 10-12.

Perkinson, James W. *White Theology: Outing Supremacy in Modernity*. New York: Palgrave MacMillan, 2004.

Rasmussen, Birgit Brander, et al., eds. *The Making and Unmaking of Whiteness*. Durham, NC: Duke University Press, 2001.

Stenschke, Christoph W. *Luke's Portrayal of Gentiles Prior to their Coming to Faith*. Tübingen: Mohr Siebeck, 1999.

Taylor, Justin, S.M. "Jerusalem Decrees." *New Testament Studies* 47 no. 3 (July 2001): 372-80.

Wall, Robert W. "The Acts of the Apostles." *The New Interpreters Bible*. Nashville: Abingdon Press, 2002, 10:1-368.

Warrior, Robert Allen. "A Native American Perspective: Canaanites, Cowboys, and Indians." *Christianity and Crisis* 49, no. 12 (1989). Reprinted in *Voices from the Margin: Interpreting the Bible in the Third World*. Edited by R. S. Sugirtharajah. Maryknoll, NY: Orbis Books, 1991, 287-95.

Williams, Delores S. *Sisters in the Wilderness: The Challenge of Womanist God-Talk*. Maryknoll, NY: Orbis Books, 1993.

Wills, Lawrence M. "The Depiction of Jews in Acts." *Journal of Biblical Literature* 110, no. 4 (1991): 631-54.

Wimbush, Vincent L., ed. *African Americans and the Bible: Sacred Texts and Social Textures*. New York: Continuum, 2000.

———. *The Bible and African-Americans: A Brief History*. Facets. Minneapolis: Fortress Press, 2002.

Witherington, B. *The Acts of the Apostles: A Socio-Rhetorical Commentary*. Grand Rapids: Eerdmans, 1998.

ABOUT THE AUTHORS

Angela Bauer-Levesque is associate professor of Hebrew Bible at Episcopal Divinity School in Cambridge, Massachusetts. She is the author of numerous articles on gender and race in biblical interpretation and is currently working on a book titled *Reading While White: Strategies for Anti-Racist Biblical Interpretations.* Her earlier book, *Gender in the Book of Jeremiah,* was published by Peter Lang Publishing in 1999.

Elizabeth M. Magill is a Christian Church (Disciples of Christ) pastor and an anti-racism trainer for the Episcopal Church. She is the author of a Bible study based on the letter of James and Elsa Tamez's book *The Scandal of James* for the United Methodist Women website. Currently she is developing a book on church closings with Congregational Renewal Associates.

www.ingramcontent.com/pod-product-compliance
Lightning Source LLC
Jackson TN
JSHW081321130125
77033JS00011B/380